HAUNTED LORAIN COUNTY

ERIC DEFIBAUGH

Published by Haunted America
A Division of The History Press
Charleston, SC
www.historypress.com

Copyright © 2019 by Eric Defibaugh
All rights reserved

Front cover: From Jack Brown

First published 2019

Manufactured in the United States

ISBN 9781467143363

Library of Congress Control Number: 2019943361

Notice: The information in this book is true and complete to the best of our knowledge. It is offered without guarantee on the part of the author or The History Press. The author and The History Press disclaim all liability in connection with the use of this book.

All rights reserved. No part of this book may be reproduced or transmitted in any form whatsoever without prior written permission from the publisher except in the case of brief quotations embodied in critical articles and reviews.

To my mother, Bunice "Bea" Defibaugh. She inspired all of her kids to be readers by example, having a book in her hand in every free moment she had—of which there were few, of course, with raising seven of us. The desire to make her proud has always been a driving force in my life, and I like to believe that authoring a book would have accomplished that. I hope she can see me now.

CONTENTS

Acknowledgements	7
Introduction	9
The Robber Ghost	13
Shadow Warriors and Bandits of Cascade	17
The Whistling Lady of Skate World	22
The Lorain Lighthouse	25
The Curse of Dean Road Bridge	28
Hotel Hauntings	31
Finwood After Dark	36
Kipton's Echoes from the Past	40
The Guardian Angel of Lofton Henderson Bridge	45
Gore Orphanage: Fact and Folklore	48
The Wardrobe	58
Restless Rest Area	61
A Tale of Two Theaters	65
Daredevil of Barres Road	73
There Goes the *Calico Jack*	76
Lady of Garden Avenue	79
Spirits of the *Spirit of '76*	83
Ghost Train at Cottesbrooke Curve	90
The Caretaker	92
Saying Goodbye	94
Other Legends from around the County	98
Bibliography	109
About the Author	111

Acknowledgements

Even a book this size can be a considerable undertaking, and I will be the first to tell you that I would not have been able to pull it off without the help of some amazing people I am blessed to have in my life.

My sincerest thanks to:

First and by far most, my wife, Judy. Her organizational skills and savvy computer expertise have proven more invaluable than I could have ever anticipated. Beyond that, had it not been for her always being at my side encouraging me—on this project and in life—I would never have been nearly as successful as I am. I literally owe everything to her, and I will forever be grateful.

Alan Leiby. When it comes to knowledge of Lorain County's history, there are few who can carry this guy's water. An author of several excellent books himself, my gratitude for his willingness to share photos from his extensive collection can't be overstated.

Rita Pullen. Easily one of the kindest and most understanding people I have ever had the fortune to meet. First a neighbor, then after the passing of my own mother, a parental figure who looked after me as her own son. Her wisdom has been essential to me, and I always seek out her perspective when considering any major decision in my life, including taking on this project.

Donna and Mark Warner. The years partnering with them for Scarlet Transportation's Ghost Tours have taught me so much not only about

Acknowledgements

the paranormal but of the importance of integrity. Their disciplined approach to their investigations forces them to objectively seek out evidence to either prove or disprove a claim rather than filtering it to support a predetermined conclusion. This is a lesson that can and should be applied to all aspects of life.

Tom Adkins. The smartest and most interesting guy I know—I learn something new every time I talk to him. He's the kind of guy who is so easygoing, you completely lose track of time when engaged in a conversation with him. Tom's knowledge of the railroad history of Lorain County is unparalleled in my eyes.

Joel and Shannon Shupp. Hearts of solid gold. Volunteering the amount of time to the community that they do is nothing short of admirable. People like them make Lorain County a better place.

Joyce Rhodes. Her knowledge of the history of the Lorain Palace Theatre and the city of Lorain itself is only surpassed by her genuine enthusiasm and cheerful disposition. She is an absolute gem in Lorain County's crown.

Jack Brown. His willingness to share his knowledge of photographic equipment and its use has opened so many possibilities to me in my endeavors. And his willingness to lend me some equipment from time to time has allowed me to take some decent photos.

The Lorain and Elyria Public Library Systems. A tremendous resource for any research project, particularly the new microfilm systems, and a quiet place to work when you need to remove yourself from the distractions of home. I found the branches of both systems to be full of friendly faces that were always happy to help.

And the good people of the Spirit of '76 Museum—one of the most important historical institutions in Lorain County. Barb, Tim, Cindy and the rest work ridiculously hard and sacrifice personally for the important task of preserving the history of the southern part of the county. They deserve acknowledgement and recognition from every resident in Lorain County.

INTRODUCTION

*But I do believe in the paranormal,
that there are things our brains just can't understand.*
—Art Bell

Ghosts. A subject that can generate both scoffs and reverence in equal parts. Books, newspaper articles, television shows, radio programs, movies, campfire stories—some tongue-in-cheek, some not—all fuel the fire of public interest and generate revenue. Some variation of "are they real?" is a question forever on the minds of the sceptics. The answer is that they are certainly real to the people who have had the experiences. Sure, there are hoaxes out there. When attention, notoriety and money are a factor in any situation, there will be people who are more than willing to game the system to get their piece. These stories tend to fall apart quickly under even the slightest of scrutiny—especially in the minds of the doubters—even lies can be based in truth. But what if the credibility of the source is beyond question? Well-respected actor on screen and stage, Patrick Stewart alleges to have seen a ghost while he was performing *Waiting for Godot* at the Theatre Royal Haymarket. Former United States congressman and Cleveland mayor Dennis Kucinich claims to have personally experienced a UFO sighting. Teddy Roosevelt, twenty-sixth President of the United States and founder of the Sierra Club, once wrote about his encounter with a Sasquatch. Would you be able to look a man as accomplished and formidable as TR in the eye and question his

Introduction

integrity? I know I couldn't. It's my belief that somewhere between Teddy Roosevelt and the hoaxes is where most ghost stories lie.

Credibility is important. When we set out developing the Ghost Tours of Lorain County for Scarlet Transportation & Adventure Tours, we knew that our success would hinge on the authenticity of our sources and the plausibility of the story of each location. That is the same approach I took with this book. Many of the stories you will find within these pages originate from solid sources such as clergy members, teachers, law enforcement officers, local businessmen, respected community elders and the like—people with good reputations and the respect of the community. These are people with something to lose, perhaps not as much as a president or a governor, but enough that I feel confident putting my own name on their word.

The rest is my perspective on the legendary folklore we all grew up hearing. In reading these particular stories, you may find some differences from the version you heard growing up—maybe a detail is out of place, maybe the location is different. Maybe more. I assure you that I have combed through every possible piece of documentation I could get my hands on for the subject, and for some of these stories—Gore Orphanage in particular—there are hundreds of documents. It can be tedious work, but when you do this, you'll find there is something akin to the game of telephone at play. With each passing generation, some details can be exaggerated ridiculously while others fade into oblivion, leaving us with a tale that vaguely resembles its origins. It's human nature to exaggerate—we all want to impress our friends—but I feel that it's important to remain as grounded as possible to maintain credibility. That's why I have done my level best to bring you not just a collection of ghost stories but a haunted history of Lorain County that has surrounded, and in some ways shaped, our community for generations. I sincerely hope you enjoy.

Let's start with a brief history of Lorain County.

In late December 1822, the state of Ohio authorized the creation of Lorain County. Located in northern Ohio, it was originally a portion of three separate counties, Huron, Medina and Cuyahoga, all part of the Connecticut Western Reserve. It was once believed that Lorain County was named for the Lorraine region of France, but given that the original proposed name for the county was Colerain, it's more likely that the name was just shortened for some unknown reason. Lorain County covers 491 square miles of land with a population of 301,356 as of the 2010 census. The city of Elyria is the county seat and the second-largest community in the county with 55,953 residents in 2000. The county averages 577 residents per square mile.

INTRODUCTION

With its northern border lying on Lake Erie, Lorain County has a rich history indelibly tied to the water. Shipbuilding along the mouth of the Black River was one of the primary industries of the county in its early years, but it was railroads that delivered rapid growth to its largest city, Lorain. First came the Cleveland Lorain & Wheeling Railroad, completed in 1873, then the Nickle Plate line in the 1880s. With the increased traffic of coal and iron ore from Lake Erie, the railroads opened the door for both economic and population growth. By the early twentieth century, steel became a major industry in Lorain County, thanks to Thomas Johnson building his steel mill along the western bank of the Black River in Lorain. Supporting industries sprang up all over the county, including Johnson's interurban rail lines to provide workers and their families access to the new steel plant. By the middle of the century, in spite of being overwhelmingly rural with only 7 percent of the county considered urban, most of Lorain County's residents would earn their livings by working in industrial manufacturing, sales or service positions.

Abolition had a very strong foothold in Lorain County, as many of the county's earliest white settlers, mostly of German, Irish and English descent, were opposed to slavery. Several buildings within the county had been used as stops on the Underground Railroad, including the Lorain County Metropark's Burrell Homestead in Sheffield Village as well as private homes in Elyria and Oberlin. After anti-slavery activists freed a runaway slave in 1858 in an episode now known as the Oberlin-Wellington Rescue, Oberlin was given the title of "The town that started the Civil War."

Oberlin also has the distinction of being home to one of the most renowned private liberal arts colleges in the United States, Oberlin College. Founded as the Oberlin Collegiate Institute in 1833 by John Jay Shipherd and Philo Stewart, it is celebrated as the first institution of higher education in the United States to admit African Americans (1835) and women (1837) into the same classes as white men. The school's Oberlin Conservatory of Music is the oldest continuously operating conservatory in the United States. Oberlin College has graduated sixteen Rhodes Scholars, twenty Truman Scholars, three Nobel Laureates and seven MacArthur fellows since its founding. A list of the school's more famous alumni includes soldier, geologist and explorer of the United States West Major John Wesley Powell; comedic actor and producer Ed Helms; singer-songwriter Liz Phair; and Moses Fleetwood Walker, who is widely credited with being the first black man to play in Major League Baseball in 1904.

The county is also home to Amherst, with its vast quarries of sandstone. During the peak of the clastic sedimentary rock's demand, Amherst was

Introduction

known as the "Sandstone Center of the World." Not to be outdone, the village of Wellington on the southern end of the county held the title of "Cheese Empire of the Nation" for four decades at the end of the nineteenth century. With more than forty cheese factories in the area, Wellington's population more than doubled in the timespan.

Notable people born in Lorain County include Ohio's forty-second governor Myron T. Herrick, U.S. Navy admiral Ernest King, astronaut Robert F. Overmyer, three-time Olympic gold medalist Tianna Bartoletta and Ohio State Buckeye and NFL linebacker Matt Wilhelm. Scientist Charles Martin Hall, artist Archibald M. Willard and the first African American to serve in the U.S. Congress, Hiram Rhodes Revels, were also well-known residents of the county. Author Toni Morrison grew up in the city of Lorain, and national champion football coach Les Miles was raised in Elyria.

The Robber Ghost

On the western edge of North Ridgeville, where the town still clings to its farming roots, stands a building that was once considered to be one of the most haunted in the county. What now contains the office of a home builder, a computer repair shop and some other small businesses, was once a large farmhouse. And this house has quite the past.

As the story goes, in the early 1900s a string of burglaries took place in the area in a relatively short amount of time. Local law enforcement had no solid leads, and the community became restless with worry. One farmer who lived out on Center Ridge Road made a pact with himself to not fall victim to such a craven crime. He worked as hard as any man to build a life for his family, and there was little he would not do to protect them and their home. Should these cowards choose to enter his house in the dead of night, he would certainly have something to say about it.

It wasn't long before the bandits made his home their next target. As with the other houses in the area, their plan was to silently slip in, take anything of value on the first floor that they could carry and get out long before the slumbering family upstairs ever knew anyone was there. To better their prospects, they chose this night specifically because of a snow storm that had begun that evening. They believed it would blind any pursuers as they made their escape, and the falling snow would cover their tracks. The plan was almost perfect. They seemed to have taken every possibility into account—every possibility except one: the family's English shepherd. The dog was aware of their presence before they had even reached the house, and it alerted the sleeping farmer. By the time the would-be burglars made it through the door, the farmer had loaded his coach gun and taken position at the top landing of the stairs—a mere twenty feet away and directly in front of the doorway. With his sight trained on the two men as they entered the room and closed the door behind them, he cocked his weapon and said with a firm voice, "Get out of my house."

He caught the bandits by surprise, and their hesitation proved fatal. After a few seconds with no visible sign of the two men heeding his command, the farmer opened fire. He hit one with the first shot, killing the man instantly. The next shot aimed at the second intruder missed its exact mark but did not miss entirely. At the sound of the first shot, he had turned and opened the door to run for his life. That heavy wooden door partially shielded him from the second shot. He leapt from the house, bleeding but alive, and disappeared into the woods to the north. His body was found later that spring in the crook of a tree, either having bled out or frozen to death.

Fast forward to 1961. Young Rita Diederich was awaked sometime in the night by a commotion at the old farmhouse across the street. She sprang from her bed to take a look out the window, worried about her friends who lived there. Her first thought was a housefire, but she saw no smoke or any sign of the fire department.

The farmhouse, still a private residence, housed two families at this time. The stairs split at a landing, giving way to two half sets of stairs that led in opposite directions to separate areas of the second floor. Mother, father and two sons lived on one side, while their daughter and her young family lived on the other. As Rita watched intently from her window, she counted the people who had gathered outside. Brothers Ron and Fred where there, as was their older sister Karen holding her infant son. Their mom was standing next to the boys, while their dad and Karen's husband were circling to the back of the house. If not a fire, Rita thought from across the street, what could have chased everyone out of the house at this hour? The answer is almost more terrifying than a fire.

It wasn't smoke or a dangerous odor or an earthquake. What chased those poor people from their beds and out onto the lawn was…screams—loud, repeating, blood-curdling screams. It was as if some prankster was in the next room with an air horn letting off repeated blasts, except this didn't sound like an air horn. It sounded like a human screaming in anguish. Both households had been awaked by this terrifying sound. At first, they thought it originated from the daughter's room, but a brief search of the room and the rest of the house resulted in nothing that could be a source. In fact, the volume seemed to be the same in every part of the house, as if the screams were emanating from the structure itself. Until they could figure out what was going on, they decided the best and safest place for them to be was outside. Even after they were outside, the screams could still be heard. After a few moments, the building fell silent. As abruptly as it started, the sound just stopped, leaving a confused and terrified group of people out in the yard.

Though the place certainly had its share of strange occurrences during their time there, this is the first time anyone had felt truly frightened. Objects disappearing from one part of the house and reappearing days later in a completely different part of the house, the sound of hurried footsteps down the second-floor hallway when no one else was home and the sliding doors on the outbuilding that were too heavy for wind to move slammed closed, all left people scratching their heads. This was different. They weren't curious about the screams; they were terrified of them.

As dawn broke, the house now silent for more than an hour, the group reluctantly entered the house. Though it was some time before they truly felt comfortable in their own home, eventually things went back to normal. Aside from occasional phantom footsteps and a mysteriously relocated object or two, they lived in relative peace for the duration of their time on the property.

Two decades later, in 1982, the house drew the attention of famed ghost hunter and psychic Norm Gauthier—founder of the Society of Psychic Research. Coming all the way from Manchester, New Hampshire, Gauthier had been brought to Cleveland to be a guest on Channel Five's *Morning Exchange*. He became aware of the house during his appearance on the *Steve Cannon Show* on WGAR-AM, when Mrs. Josephine Diederich, mother of Rita, had called into the show to share the stories of the old farmhouse across the street. Gauthier agreed that it would be worth investigating. Arrangements were made with the Group W. Cable Company, which had converted the old house into their local station headquarters, for the psychic and all of his investigating gadgets to spend a night.

Mr. Gauthier was accompanied on the investigation by Tab Berg, producer and director for the cable company, and Terry Trakas, local origination director for Group W, who informed Norm of some of the more current happenings on the property. Among the usual mysterious relocation of objects and occasional random sounds from the second floor, they shared with him a new and curious detail. When the cable company took possession of the building, there had been a strange and seemingly useless mound in the middle of the basement's dirt floor. The space was to be used to store various types of equipment, so they had decided to level the mound. A few days after completing the task, an employee discovered that the mound had returned. Assuming that another employee had played a joke on him, the man grabbed a shovel and leveled the area once more. He was the last to leave the building that evening and the first to arrive the following day. Once inside, he immediately went down to the basement to retrieve something out of storage. To his astonishment, he was greeted by the same mound he had twice leveled, at approximately the same height and exactly in the same location. When no one was able to offer a reasonable explanation, it was decided to leave the mound in place. Whatever it was, that mound was determined to stay.

After the investigation, Norm Gauthier took his evidence back to **WGAR-AM**. For years afterwards, every October Steve Cannon would play on the air the sounds he recorded that night. The audio clips included a voice that said, "I'm here," a low, agonizing moan and a dog barking. The most chilling of all was the sound of what seemed to be the cocking of a gun followed by a clear and firm voice commanding, "Get out of my house."

Shadow Warriors and Bandits of Cascade

Near the center of the county seat of Elyria lies the town's largest and most popular park, Cascade. The 135-acre park is situated around a ravine carved by the same glaciers that produced the Great Lakes. The confluence of its east and west branches forms the main body of the Black River within the park where it continues to flow northward through the ravine as a tributary to Lake Erie. The park features rock formations, hiking trails, two impressive waterfalls and spectacular autumn foliage. Now managed by the Lorain County Metro Parks, the rugged walls of the ravine, along with its open green spaces, make Cascade the perfect place for family recreation.

In the 1700s, the Black River was known as the "Reneshoua River" and later in that century was also referred to as "la Riviere de la Cuiliere" by early European explorers. The origin of those names is uncertain, although "Cuilliere" was also the name of a French fur trader who frequented the Lake Erie shore areas around 1760. Nineteenth-century historians misidentified the Black River as the "Canesadooharie," which was thought to translate roughly to "black pearl," or even more romantically, as "string of black pearls." Thereafter, the river was known as the Black River. The actual Canesadooharie was likely the Huron River, which had been written about, along with his visit to the "falls," by Colonel James Smith, who had been captured by Native Americans and brought to live with them near Sandusky Bay.

Cascade Park in Elyria. *From the author.*

The region's indigenous peoples found this area to be an ideal place to settle with its freshwater supply and wild game, such as elk, deer, bear, wolves and turkeys, to sustain them. Tribal wars over the region had all but annihilated the once-powerful Erie people, and by 1755, the Wyandots were the last-known Native Americans to occupy Cascade Park prior to the European settlers. Those who have ever been in the park after dark are convinced that members of the tribe still hunt those grounds.

People have reported seeing dark shadows on and near the park's swing sets. Witnesses have also reported the sound of a bipedal animal crossing the river in front of them even though the water's current remained undisturbed. Others have observed the glow of fire reflecting onto the rugged façade of the ravine near the north falls. Shadowy figures were said to be moving about in the glow, as if they were dancing around a ceremonious fire. Though witnesses have tried to locate the source of the light, it seemed as they got closer, the glow would fade into the darkness. With the alarming thought of vandals in the park, one tenacious group of people made it all the way down to where they thought the light originated—in a small nook in the shale formations adjacent to the river. They searched around the immediate area, but they never found an explanation for the glow they saw.

Once on a spring night, an aspiring photographer was on the observation deck built above the river trying to get the perfect shot of the falls lit by a full moon. He was just about to start shooting when he heard an unexpected sound coming from the general area where he had parked his car moments earlier. The low, rhythmic beating of a drum, like something you'd hear in an old western film, seemed out of place in this part of the country. At first, he thought it was children playing in the park, but he looked down at his watch and realized that it was nearly midnight. Concern for his car compelled him to pack up his camera gear and make his way back down the path toward the parking lot. As he moved through the darkness, he thought he caught movement to his left in his peripheral vision. He stopped and turned his body to get a better look but saw nothing. After a few seconds he started down the path again. Another fifteen yards or so down the trail, he saw movement a second time, but now the movement was on his right. On alert, he snapped his head in that direction, without stopping this time. Again, he saw nothing but trees and shadows in the darkness. Quickening his pace, he was beginning to think his mind was playing tricks on him, when he thought he saw the dark silhouette of a man passing from behind one tree to another off to his left. He heard a twig snap a few feet behind him, and in that instant, he knew someone—or something—was stalking him in the darkness. He didn't even turn his head to try to get a look at what had made the noise—he just sprinted down the path. By the time he reached his car, he was in a panic. He made it out of the park, though he was sure he wouldn't.

Some believe that whatever lurks in the nighttime darkness in Cascade Park is more than a roaming band of Wyandot spirit hunters. They say that the souls of local bandits are searching for their illicit goods allegedly hidden in the park. The caves, nooks and crevasses in the rock within the park proved to be a suitable hideout for outlaws and a perfect place to

Falls Overlook in Cascade Park. *From the author.*

hide ill-gotten goods. Once referred to by locals as the Robbers' Den, the stone outcroppings were used as a covert transfer point for a counterfeiting operation in the area.

And then there was story of Blinky Morgan and his gang. One of northern Ohio's most notorious bad guys, Blinky, and his company of desperados, stole a large quantity of valuable furs from Benedict and Ruedy, a downtown Cleveland department store, in January 1887. It is known that after the heist, the bandits hid out from the law for a period of time in Robbers' Den. They allegedly stashed their stolen merchandise in the rock formations and decided to sneak out of the state until the attention from the cops wore off. After killing one Cleveland police officer and severely injuring another at the train station in Ravenna, Ohio, the gang was finally captured in Alpena, Michigan, on June 28. To this day, no one is sure what became of the stolen furs.

Perhaps the mysterious figures that have been spotted in Cascade over the decades are members of Blinky's gang who have returned to claim their buried treasure. Or maybe there's still one last strongbox full of counterfeit bills still buried somewhere waiting to be picked up, and the dark figures looming in the darkness intend on doing just that.

Or, since being in the park after sunset is prohibited by law, another possibility is that it's just a mischievous park ranger attempting to scare you away.

Robbers' Den in Cascade Park. *From the author.*

Above: Robbers' Den in Cascade Park. *From the author*.

Left: Robbers' Den in Cascade Park. *From the author*.

The Whistling Lady of Skate World

Back in the days before the Interstate Highway System, U.S. Route 6 running along Lake Erie through Lorain County was a major freight lane between Cleveland and other major cities to the west. Facilities such as fuel stops, repair shops and hotels were necessary to support the tractor-trailers that hauled cargo to, from and through the region. Prior to becoming the most popular roller skating rink in the county, the building known as Lorain Skate World once served as a motel for truckers. The western portion of the building, including the skate rental room, the pro shop, both the men's and women's restrooms and the offices were all part of the original motel. It served as part of a truck-stop complex that was last called Benny's, and it provided a place where drivers could get a hot meal and catch some shuteye while their rigs were being serviced and repaired in the building next door.

The spirit that is said to wander in and around the skating rink dates back to the old motel. Allegedly, a woman was shot and died from her wounds in one of the guest rooms—now thought to be the room that serves as the game room—in the late 1950s. A lady of the night, she was gunned down by a client after her failed attempt to pocket his billfold when he stepped out to fetch some ice. On his return, he noticed that the wallet was not where he left it and an argument ensued, and he shot her with a pistol.

The mysterious woman has been spotted on multiple occasions in the years since her tragic death, roaming the hallway outside the room where she lost her life, as well as other parts of the building and even on the adjacent

Lorain Skate World. *From the author.*

Railroad tracks behind Skate World. *From the author.*

properties surrounding Skate World. But usually she is heard rather than seen. It turns out this unique spirit is quite the whistler, and she often makes her presence known with a melodic, high-pitched tune. On at least one occasion she was seen standing by the dumpster behind the building after one poor fellow curiously sought out the source of the whistling.

The man first heard the melodic sounds coming from the back of the building as he got out of his car one cold winter day. As he came around the corner to the north side of the building, he stopped dead in his tracks, startled by the sight of a woman who was underdressed for the weather. She was standing with her back to him—facing the lake to the north, whistling her tune. Wondering if she was in distress, he asked if she was in need of help. There was no reply, as she just continued whistling and staring out over the icy waters of the Great Lake. Assuming she had not heard him the first time, he asked louder and started to walk over to her as he spoke. To his astonishment, by the time his third step hit the ground, the woman vanished. She dissipated into the breeze like a puff of smoke—her whistling fading away along with her. Frozen in confusion for a few seconds, the man shook his head and spun around, headed back to his car and pulled out of the parking lot. It would be twenty years before he ever told a soul about what happened that day.

The Lorain Lighthouse

On October 22, 1913, Congress granted authorization for the allocation of $35,000 for a permanent light and fog signal at the mouth of the Black River in Lorain. The United States Corps of Engineers began construction of the "Jewell of the Port" in 1916. By the end of June, the following year, the concrete base was in place, the steel work had been erected and the reinforced concrete walls were finished, allowing a temporary acetylene light to shine atop the new structure. A modern fourth-order Fresnel lens, manufactured by Macbeth-Evans Lens Company of Pittsburgh to produce five seconds of light followed by a five-second eclipse, commenced operation atop the new lighthouse on April 7, 1919.

The lighthouse is a sturdy, stout structure built to withstand the fury of Lake Erie at its worst. Standing fifty-eight feet above the water, its walls of reinforced concrete are thirty-two inches thick at the basement level and taper to ten inches at the top floor. The basement level held a cistern, coal bin and storage space. A power room, bathroom and tool room are located on the first floor, while a living room, galley with pantry, bunkroom and air tanks for the foghorns are located on the second floor. The third floor had space for the diaphones, a timing device, a spare parts locker, foghorns, a seven-hundred-gallon water tank and stairs leading to the lantern room. The first year lightkeepers lived on the premises was 1919.

The Lighthouse Service had been responsible for the upkeep and maintenance of all lighthouses and light vessels in the United States until 1939, when President Theodore Roosevelt ordered that the authority of all U.S. lighthouses be absorbed by the United States Coast Guard. Three men at a time from the local Coast Guard unit would be stationed at the Lorain Lighthouse. They would also occasionally serve as lookouts for both a lifeboat station and the air force.

As part of a $22 million improvement of the harbor at Lorain, an outer breakwall was put in place, and an automated modern tower at its western tip took over the function of lighting the harbor entrance in 1965. No longer needed, the forty-nine-year-old lighthouse was slated for demolition. A $25,000 contract was awarded to the Great Lakes Dredge and Dock Company to tear down the building in October 1965. After an inspection, the demolition company increased their requirement for the project to $75,000 due to the thirty-two inches of reinforced concrete basement walls. This price increase was rejected by the Coast Guard and the structure survived the close call. Eventually, the Coast Guard decommissioned the lighthouse and it was turned over to the General Services Administration, which awarded the Lorain Lighthouse deed to the Lorain County Historical Society in exchange for $1 on the condition that it be operated and maintained as a historical landmark. In December 1978, the Lorain Lighthouse was placed in the National Register of Historic Places. County residents have been marveling at its charm and tenacity ever since.

Viewing the majestic lighthouse from anywhere along Lorain's lakeshore, one cannot help but admire its tranquil beauty. Its image has been used countless times in models, paintings, postcards, t-shirts, logos, pins, needlework projects, posters and has even graced the cover of the Lorain County phonebook. But even an icon such as this can hold secrets, and the legend of the ghost of the Lorain Lighthouse has persisted throughout its history.

The story goes that during the original construction in 1916, a worker fell into a cavity in the foundation of the structure and was knocked unconscious. None of his coworkers noticed his sudden absence, and without any knowledge of his whereabouts, they continued their work for the day. Concrete was poured into the cavity, entombing the man alive. Doomed to spend an eternity in the concrete tomb, some believe that he now strolls the halls of the lighthouse, as if he doesn't know that he is dead and is trying to finish his work.

During the years the lighthouse was abandoned and shuttered, many witnesses aboard passing boats saw what appeared to be the dark shape of a man moving around the platform at the base of the building at twilight. Fishermen who had climbed out on the break wall for a better position to cast their lines have claimed to have heard the sound of a hammer pounding a chisel coming from within the lighthouse. In more recent years, visitors taking tours of the lighthouse have heard whispers while in the basement that seem to be saying, "Find me."

Some have speculated that the spirit wandering those hallways is someone entirely different. The ill-fated construction worker was not the only soul lost at that location. Prior to the construction of the lighthouse that exists today, the position was known as the Black River Light Station. This station was a cylindrical brick tower capped with a lantern room and was located at the end of the pier that extended from the west bank of the Black River. The tower had eight lamps fueled by lard oil, and since there were no living quarters on the pier, the oil would have to be carried out each day. Upon examining the Black River Light Station in 1838, Lieutenant Charles T. Platt of the U.S. Navy noted,

> *The beacon stands on the west pier, which extends 680 feet into the lake. In order to render it safe for the tender (keeper) to approach the beacon in foul weather, it will be necessary to raise the pier at least two feet. At three different times last year, such was the violence of the waves, that persons endeavoring to light the beacon were washed from the pier, one of whom was drowned.*

Whether it's a construction worker from more than a hundred years ago attempting to complete his work or a seventeenth-century lighthouse keeper fulfilling his duties, it is quite likely that this historic structure has never been truly abandoned.

The Curse of Dean Road Bridge

Running north to south, following Lorain County's western border in Florence Township is a two-lane country thoroughfare called Dean Road. Beginning at Sperry Road on the north end, the narrow rural route forms a relatively straight line as it heads south until it reaches the crossing of the Vermilion River at Dean's Hollow. After a couple tight turns that drop you into Dean's Hollow toward the river, you find yourself at the footing of the Dean Road Bridge.

As with its more famous upriver neighbor, Swift Hollow, Dean's Hollow and the bridge that spans the river there carry a certain ominous weight in the air. Even without knowing the legend that lurks there, you still get the feeling that something dreadful has taken place. And indeed, it has.

Spanning 171 feet, the historic Pratt truss bridge was originally built in 1898 by the Massillon Bridge Company of—you guessed it—Massillon, Ohio, and served as the area's main crossing point of the Vermilion River well into the twentieth century. It was deemed to be of enough historic significance by the National Park Service that it was added to the National Register of Historic Places on November 28, 1978. In spite of the bridge's beautiful natural setting, locals will tell you the bridge has a dark past that still lingers to this day.

One day long ago, a local man had made the decision to end his life. Whether it was his intention is unclear, but of all the possible methods of accomplishing this ghastly deed, he chose a way that would be sure to send a message to his neighbors. He found a length of rope, tied one end into

Dean Road Bridge. *From the author.*

a noose and made his way to the bridge in Dean's Hollow. Once there, he climbed up a truss and onto the crossbeams that span across the bridge directly above the roadway. After securing the other end of the rope to one of the crossbeams, he slipped the noose around his neck and leapt to his death. His body hung there, suspended just a few feet off of the deck, for three full days before it was discovered. After the body was identified by the authorities, his death was promptly ruled a homicide. He was carried off and interred in a nearby cemetery, the whereabouts of which are now lost to history.

Years later, as the memory of the incident had all but faded from the minds of the locals, a respected elder of the community told his neighbor about seeing a noose hanging from the bridge as he crossed at dusk the previous night. After the neighbor went to investigate and found no sign of a noose or anything else hanging from the bridge, it was dismissed as a juvenile prank and no one gave the incident a second thought. There are people in every community with a distasteful sense of humor, after all, and theirs was no different. When the elderly man was found dead on his front porch later that evening, no one made the connection. At his age, it was assumed to be a heart attack. The following year, a much younger man, a hand from a nearby dairy farm, made a similar claim about seeing a noose hanging overhead as he crossed the bridge, and by the end of the day he had been found dead in a barn. This time judging by his wounds, it was determined that he had been gored to death by the bull he had recently brought in for breeding. A strange accident, but still no one seemed to connect the dots.

By the time a third mysterious death had occurred a few months later, people finally began to recognize the disturbing pattern. It was revealed that this victim had also seen the noose hanging from the bridge. Soon after, the custom was adopted to look anywhere but up at the crossbeams as you make your way across the bridge—a custom that many still adhere to today. For it is understood that should you catch a glimpse of that dreadful noose, it could mean the end is near.

Little is known about the man who took his own life on that bridge so long ago, but it is believed that his soul was so greatly tormented that even his death wasn't enough to alleviate his suffering. So, he lingers, seeking out fellow troubled souls to take from this life as retribution for his eternal suffering. Even now, should you find yourself crossing the Dean Road Bridge, it is recommended that you keep your gaze on the road ahead of you or even toward the river on either side—anywhere but up. You know, just to be safe.

Hotel Hauntings

In the summer of 1955, three men boarded a Piper PA-22-160 helicopter and set out to scout the areas surrounding the recently completed Ohio Turnpike. Two of the men, Kemmons Wilson and Wallace E. Johnson, chartered the chopper and its pilot to get a bird's-eye view of the terrain in search of potential sites for the expansion of their hotel chain. The exits of the new highway provided excellent opportunities for hotel locations, and exit 8 in Elyria offered access to the area's industrial juggernauts, such as U.S. Steel and the American Ship Building Company, along with the growing automobile assembly industry. This made it an optimal location. In just a couple of years, the construction would be completed on the new Holiday Inn in Elyria—one of the original 10 of a chain that went on to number more than 1,400 globally, at its peak.

Beginning in the late 1970s, a series of strange and seemingly random occurrences began to take place at the hotel—some witnessed by guests, others by employees and all without explanation. The following are the various accounts over the years.

One guest told a story of what happened during an extended stay while he was working on a large project in Elyria. On random days when he came back to his room after his work day, the television would be on when he opened the door. As soon as he walked into the room, the television would instantly turn off as if someone else was in the room with the remote control. Sometimes he would stand at the door waiting, and the television would stay on until he entered the room. This happened so frequently that he finally asked to change rooms for the remainder of his stay.

Sometime in 1989, after spending several days at the hotel, a man was awakened by a phone call in the middle of the night on the last night of his stay. He answered it groggily. The front desk was calling, saying something along the lines of, "Sorry to wake you, but we've been receiving a couple of reports about rooms being broken into and some stuff being stolen. We are calling to make sure you locked your door and are safe." The weary guest replied that he was fine and hung up the phone. He decided to double-check that he locked the door. As he sat up in the bed, he noticed that the door to his room was ajar. Now on alert, he cautiously checked the room and found that nothing was missing, and there was no sign of anyone else in the room. Just to be certain, he slowly approached the door, opened it slightly and peeked out. Sitting on the floor right outside his room was his shaving kit. Looking in both directions up and down the hallway, he reached out and grabbed it before quickly closing and locking the door.

After he calmed down a bit, he called down to the front desk and said, "Hey, you just called me about the break-ins around the hotel, and I just want to report that my room was broken into while I was sleeping. Nothing was stolen and I am fine. I figured you would like to know."

The front desk replied, "You must be mistaken, sir. We never called your room, and we haven't received any reports of break-ins."

Just past midnight on a quiet Tuesday, a security guard who worked at the Holiday Inn in the 90s had to use the restroom after making his rounds. This bathroom he decided to use is in a public area near the front desk. It was quiet, and he was fairly certain that he was the only one in the room when he entered. As he walked up to the urinal and began to relieve himself, he heard a fast-paced knocking sound—like someone rapping with their knuckles—coming from the stalls behind him. He looked over his shoulder and saw the door for the handicap stall was vibrating, which he decided was the source of the knocking sound. The door was moving as if someone had locked it from the inside and was bouncing it between the lock and the outer doorstop. As the security guard finished up, he turned and faced the door, which was still making the noise. He briefly thought that it could be a coworker playing a prank, so he forced out a laugh and said, "Very funny." It immediately stopped. He then walked over to the door, expecting it to be locked with a coworker inside. He raised his hand to knock, and when his knuckles made contact with the door, it swung wide open. No one was inside. He could not find an explanation for why the door would have made that noise on its own.

A campaign manager in her mid-thirties was staying at the hotel during the 1998 campaign season when she had a strange encounter in her room on the fifth floor. While deep in thought at the desk in the room working on the next day's schedule, she became aware of voices talking and laughing loud enough to be in the same room. When she looked up, the talking ceased. She took a brief look around the room and went back to her work. A few moments later the voices started again. The noise started softly and grew until the room sounded like a crowded hall with forty or fifty people talking all at once. She got up this time to try to locate whoever was being so disruptive, but as soon as she stood up, it was silent. She searched but found nothing making sound anywhere in the room—not the television, not the radio. She even checked the hallway for people, though she was convinced that the noise was coming from somewhere in her room, but still she found nothing. Around two o'clock in the morning, she was in bed and felt someone brush strands of hair from her forehead and tuck them behind her ear. She jumped up and turned on the light, but no one was there. She felt comfortable in her room for the three weeks she stayed there, but she got very little sleep on this night.

Across from the lobby is Mr. D's, an in-house restaurant and bar. One waitress, during her second day on the job, saw a little girl who was about four years old pop her head out of a cabinet behind the bar and look around before shrinking back inside and closing the door. The server walked around the right side of the bar—the only way in or out of the area—to locate the little girl and maybe help find her parents. When she opened the cabinet door, there was no one inside.

That wasn't the only appearance of a mischievous child. After checking in, two traveling sisters headed up to their room. One decided to hop in the shower while the other unpacked her luggage. As she stood at the foot of the bed going through a suitcase, she heard tiny footsteps near the bathroom door. She stopped what she was doing to concentrate on the sound. She heard the footsteps again—this time they seemed to be coming toward her and stopping directly in front of the gap between the two beds where she stood. After a few seconds she gathered the nerve to ask whatever it was, "Are you there?" She immediately felt embarrassed as she realized that the sounds were likely just a kid running around out in the hallway. Then she heard a little girl's giggle right in front of her.

Even the housekeeping staff had their share of creepy experiences in the hotel. There was one room on the second floor at the end of the hall where things would happen while the housekeepers were working on preparing it for the next guests. It seemed the same two things would happen every time one of them was working in that room. The first and most common was that the faucet would start to run—not full blast, but it would turn on enough to run steadily. The employee would be changing the bedsheets in the other room and suddenly hear water gurgling down the drain. Sometimes they would be cleaning the tub and shower and hear it turn on behind them.

The other odd thing that would happen in this particular room was that the television would turn on while they were cleaning the room. It was common for the housekeepers to be making the bed and rustling the sheets, then suddenly hear the sound of muffled voices before turning to see that the television had turned on with its volume turned down low. This would only happen once during the cleaning. Once the set was powered off again, it would stay off.

Though they never felt threatened in any way, the employees always felt as though they were being watched in that room. Many of the staff felt as though it was someone trying to reach out, and whoever it was had simply had a limited way to do it. Some of them even tried to communicate back by saying hello or apologizing for not understanding the message they were trying to send.

After a long drive from Baltimore, a steel industry consultant by the name of Benjamin Braxton was looking forward to a hot meal and a good night's sleep. As he checked in at the front desk, the woman behind the desk explained to him that the room next to his was undergoing some repairs and there may be some noises associated with the construction during the daytime hours. This would be of no concern to Ben. He had a long day of meetings the following day at the plant in Lorain and would be hitting the road afterward, so wouldn't be around for it anyway. He thanked her and headed up to his room on the third floor. After freshening up he decided to go back out to grab a late dinner.

As he opened the door, he heard a loud bang from the room next door. It's half past seven in the evening—not exactly daytime hours he thought to himself, looking down at his watch. He moved out to the hallway, and just as he reached the door to the adjacent room, he heard anther loud bang that stopped him in his tracks. Curious, he decided to take a peek at the room through the peephole in the door. As he did so, he saw that the room was illuminated by the parking lot lights through the window on the far wall, and to his surprise, it didn't seem to be under construction at all. In fact, aside from the curtains hanging around the window, the room was completely empty.

Ninety minutes later, Ben returned to the hotel after his dinner at the Midway Tavern. As he walked down the hall toward his room, he started thinking about the room adjacent to his. If the room was empty, what was making the banging noises? He must have missed something, he thought to himself and decided to get another look. He approached the door and leaned in to put his eye to the peephole. He suddenly leaned back, not quite understanding what he was seeing. He checked the room number to make sure he was at the same door as earlier, and after confirming that he was, he shook his head and looked through the peephole again. Unlike before, he couldn't see the window or the curtains or the room at all. This time, all he could see was the color red, like someone had blocked the peephole with construction paper.

Sufficiently weirded out now, he decided to forget the whole thing and call it a night.

The following morning, he was checking out when curiosity again got the best of him and he casually asked the manager behind the desk about the repairs in the next room. The manager sighed and said, "Truthfully? We don't rent out that room anymore. So many people have complained to us that we just save ourselves the trouble and tell guests that room is under construction."

"What sort of complaints do they have?" the man asked.

"As strange as it sounds, they all say it's haunted by a ghost with red eyes."

Finwood After Dark

"I can't believe it's almost midnight already," Joel thought to himself as he passed through the last room of the house, turning off the lights as he made his way to the door. It had been another unexpectedly long night working out the kinks of his electric train displays. Five of the eight tracks had taken turns all night calling for his attention, all while about eight hundred people passed by on their way into the house, many of them stopping to pick his brain about his trains. In the nearly twenty years he has been doing this, he couldn't remember the trains being quite this finicky.

It started with his father nearly thirty years ago. The property had been left to the city of Elyria for public use by the estate of Judge Guy B. Findley. It was named Finwood Estate in his honor. The beautiful Tudor-style house sits on a wooded forty-one-acre lot overlooking a ravine. Aside from the decorative woodwork and paneling inside, the judge had the entire home constructed with cement and bricks. The Parks and Recreation Department almost immediately began using the property as a rental facility for private parties, mostly to draw enough revenue to keep it from becoming a financial liability for the city. It also hosted a very special resident in December: Santa Claus.

For years, every night from the first of December until Christmas Eve, the residents of Elyria and the surrounding communities have been enjoying the massive holiday displays as much as the opportunity to take a photo with the big guy himself. Among the most popular features of that display have been the electric trains of Joel Walter Shupp. Donating both his time and

Finwood Estates in Elyria. *From the author.*

his prized equipment, Joel Walter spent his days leading up to the season setting up an elaborate track system, including building tunnels and bridges spanning both sides of the sidewalk leading up to the home's entry door. He would then spend the rest of the season maintaining the display and answering questions from hundreds of wide-eyed visitors, old and young. Joel and his trains soon became as much of a tradition as Santa himself.

It wasn't long before his son, Joel Martin, got in on the action. Sharing his father's passion for the trains was never an issue for Joel Martin, but time was another story. He wasn't a retiree like his father—far from it. He had a more-than-full-time job as an accountant and a family of his own to fill his days. Over time Joel began to realize how important the train display was not only to his father but to the community as a whole. So, each year as his father aged, Joel Martin and his wife, Shannon, would take more and more off his father's shoulders until the inevitable day came when it was finally time for Joel Walter to "retire" again. From that point on, it would be Joel Martin and Shannon's show to put on.

Joel Martin had always been aware of the strange things that would sometimes occur at Finwood. His father told him stories of his tools moving on their own from one location to another—an unlikely occurrence for a man as fastidious as his father was known to be. Joel Martin had seen for himself the creepy underground tunnel leading from the house to the ravine to the north and wondered if its purpose was actually for escape in the unlikely event of a house fire, as was the official explanation, or if it was for something else. He often wondered why Judge Findley's children, who had grown up in the home, wanted nothing to do with it later in life. It was a beautiful piece of property after all. Who could possibly refuse such an inheritance? Then he began having issues with his own tools. His trusty cordless DeWalt drill—the one his father had gifted him some years back—worked flawlessly every time he needed it at home, but it simply refused to come to life at Finwood. His issues were all minor annoyances—not really adding up to much. Until one night, that is.

"Did you get all the lights?" Shannan asked Joel as he pulled the key from the dead bolt and dropped the ring into his pocket.

"Yep," he said, looking down at a particularly troublesome stretch of track as he started down the sidewalk toward her. Where the hell could that short be?

"You sure about that?"

He stopped and looked up at her and saw that she was wearing that wry smile of hers—the one she showed off when he'd made a silly mistake

Finwood Estates in Elyria. *From the author.*

and she knew he was not aware of it yet. He did that often when he was distracted with a problem, and he knew it. Her eyes lifted over his head to a second-floor window of the house where a light had obviously been left on. Before he turned to see for himself, he let out a tired sigh, knowing she had him. He dropped his gaze and reached back into his pocket to retrieve the key when he heard it.

At first, he couldn't quite make it out. It was not the volume that he struggled with; the sound was plenty loud. And it was not an unfamiliar sound to him. He knew he'd heard it before, but where? It took three or four seconds for it to register with him, and it hit him like a hammer when it did. He spun around and looked up at the dimly lit window on the second floor. Sure enough, that's where the sound seemed to be coming from. He whirled back to his wife, whose wry smile had been replaced with an expression that was equal parts shock and confusion.

It wasn't uncommon for people to leave objects in the house, in fact it happened all the time. Winter hats, gloves, eyeglasses, cell phones, even an occasional purse. The lost-and-found box in the garage was teeming with forgotten items, and the pile grew almost daily. But *this*?

"Do you hear that?" she whispered, her eyes never leaving the window. "Is that a…baby?"

Joel didn't say a word. If Shannon was hearing it too, then it wasn't his weary imagination getting to him. He furiously searched for the key in his pocket as he closed the distance to the door in a flash. Almost without thinking, he unlocked the door and was inside the home, knowing exactly which room he was heading to—a left through the family room, a right down the short hall, another right to the stairs. He was on autopilot now. He made a right at the top of the stairs, ran to the first door on the left and burst in, panting from the stairs and the adrenalin rush. He scanned the room. He was so fixated on looking for signs of movement that he didn't realize that the only light in the room—the only light in the house—was coming through the window from a light in the parking lot outside. Aside from that, he was standing in a dark room completely alone.

If there is anything more terrifying than hearing a baby crying in the dark when you are absolutely certain there is no baby around, I have yet to encounter it.

Kipton's Echoes from the Past

It's hard to imagine now, but prior to the 1880s, time in the United States was very much a local issue. Almost every town in the country had kept their own time, mostly based on the position of the sun, and it could vary widely from place to place. Each town's standard time would be shown on a clock somewhere in plain view—usually on a tower or church steeple or even in a jeweler's shop window. Residents would abide by this time standard, and visitors would set their personal watches upon arrival.

It wasn't until the sprawling reach of the railroads began to push farther through the country that standardized time was finally implemented. The first man in the United States to sense the growing need for time standardization was amateur astronomer William Lambert, who presented a recommendation for the establishment of time meridians to Congress as early as 1809. The proposal was not adopted, probably because the bulk of the country at that time spread north to south, keeping a similar path of the sun. It wasn't until 1883, after a vast expansion westward by the United States, that a proposal to standardize time zones by Charles Dowd of Saratoga Springs, New York, was finally adopted by U.S. railroad companies.

Even as the new time standards were implemented across the continuously growing country, they were wholly dependent on the accuracy of town clocks and personal time pieces. Though tremendous strides had been made in the reliability of time pieces, the lack of understanding of the importance of strictly adhering to a precise schedule resulted in lax timekeeping practices by some railroad workers. When you are talking about hundreds of thousands of tons of wood, steel and people moving at speeds of up to seventy miles per hour on a fixed linear road, a discrepancy of just a few minutes could prove catastrophic. Such a catastrophe occurred in Kipton, Ohio, on April 19, 1891.

On that fateful day, forty miles west of Cleveland, Ohio, the fast mail train known as the No.14 was heading west on the Lake Shore and Michigan Southern Railroad approaching the station in Kipton. The fast mail was running at full speed, and the Toledo Express, a train consisting of five coaches and two baggage cars, was scheduled to pull over to a side track to allow the mail train to pass. The Toledo Express was four minutes behind schedule and was stopped when the two collided. The massive collision killed nine men—six of them postal clerks working on the fast mail train. The impact was so violent that more than fifty feet away, most of the depot's windows broke.

It is likely that the line of freight cars and the station itself had impaired the vision of the engineer of the mail train. Though he applied the breaks the second he saw the Toledo Express, he knew it was far too late to avoid the collision. According to the *Atlanta Journal-Constitution* article titled "A Horror of the Rail" on April 19 of that year,

> *The engine of the Toledo Express was knocked squarely across the track, and that of the fast mail reared in the air, resting on the top of the other. The fast mail consisted of three mail cars and two parlor cars, and the Toledo Express of five coaches and two baggage cars. The first and second mail cars were telescoped and smashed to kindling wood, and the third crashed into the first two and rolled over on the station platform, breaking the windows of the building.*

The six postal clerks killed in the wreck were from Ohio. They were Frank Nugent of Toledo; J.L. Clement of Cleveland; James McKinley of Conneaut; and Charles Hammil, John J. Bowerfield and Charles L. McDowell, all of Elyria. This horrific wreck made headlines across the country, and an investigation was launched immediately to determine its cause.

Initial investigators determined that the Toledo Express crew was at fault. Their train was late and should not have started out for Kipton from their previous stop in Oberlin, knowing that the fast mail was approaching on the same line. The investigation centered on the engineer's watches—one of which was found to be four minutes slow. As a result of this discovery, the general superintendent of the Lake Shore and Michigan

Southern Railroad appointed well-known Cleveland jeweler Webster C. Ball to investigate timekeeping issues on the line. Ball created a new set of standards for railroad pocket watches that included a weekly inspection and a requirement of being accurate to within thirty seconds and having fifteen jewels and a white watch face and black Arabic numbers with each minute shown. The watches were also mandated to be temperature compensated, because variations in seasonal and regional temperatures could cause a watch to speed up or slow down.

In addition, Ball required railroad engineers to have their watches inspected regularly, upon which they were issued certificates that guaranteed the watches' reliability. If an engineer's watch was found to be faulty in any way, he had to pay for the repair himself. While the watch was being repaired, he would be required to borrow a certified loan watch from the jeweler performing the repairs. Having an accurate watch would now be a requirement for the job. It was vitally important for every train to operate on a strict time standard since most railroad lines had only one track for trains traveling in both directions. The Kipton disaster proved that an error of just four minutes in such an environment could mean the difference between life and death.

Kipton, Ohio. *From the author.*

To this day, if you are known as a person who keeps an exemplary time schedule, you are said to be "on the Ball."

In the early years following the accident, there were several residents who witnessed events that were referred to as "echoes from the past" in the area around the tragic sight. Sounds of a phantom steam engine—even long after steam engines were phased out in favor of diesel engines—releasing its pressure valves, as if it had just come to a stop at the station that no longer existed, were heard multiple times by bewildered residents of Kipton. Random disembodied screams had been heard from the wooded areas surrounding the site at various times of the day. Even after the rail line was abandoned in 1975, these strange occurrences persisted in the area.

In 1992, several park districts agreed to create a series of connecting trails across the state. The North Coast Inland Trail is a work-in-progress multipurpose trail project that currently consists of several separate portions defined by their counties in northern Ohio. The initial goal was to connect all of these portions and to extend the trails into Indiana and Pennsylvania and beyond. The nonprofit organization Firelands Rails to Trails Inc. eventually gave the project the collective name "North Coast Inland Trail" (NCIT) in 2000. After years of planning and construction by the Lorain County Metroparks, on August 15, 1998, the twelve-foot-wide asphalt-paved Lorain County section of the NCIT was opened to the public. A large part of the NCIT has been constructed on defunct railroad tracks, using their elevated and relatively flat beds as optimal bases for the multipurpose trails. Much of the western section of Lorain County's portion was built on the raised bed of the old Lake Shore and Michigan Southern Railroad tracks and goes right through the crash site in Kipton.

As the county's residents increasingly visit Kipton to use the trail, more and more people have reported experiencing strange occurrences that range from minor distractions to terrifying episodes. The most common of these are the shadowy people lurking in the woods east of town. Some people have even reported seeing multiple figures at a time and some have said that these strange figures have glowing red eyes. The shadowy people just seem to be observing the people as they pass by on the trail. Another common occurrence are the random howls and screams from the same woods.

One bicyclist witnessed a light on the path as he crossed State Route 511 headed east out of Kipton as dusk settled in. He paid little attention to the light at first, as it was quite common for bikers and hikers on the path to use headlamps to light their way in the dark. As he closed in on the light, he noticed that it was lower to the ground and seemed to be swaying back and forth, as if being held by a handle—like a lantern—as opposed to being worn like a head lamp. This struck him as odd considering how unusual and dated the use of lanterns had become in modern times. He also began to detect the faint sound of a small bell ringing…ding…ding…ding. Confused, he pulled his hand brake until his bike came to a stop about twenty yards from the light. The light was still swaying back and forth, and the bell was still ringing. He squinted his eyes, trying to get a better look but was still unable to make out who or what was slowly approaching him. Just as he was about to call out, the light suddenly changed direction. Still swaying as if being carried by an invisible man, it made a hard right and headed off the asphalt toward the woods to the north. The bicyclist stood in shock as he watched the first layer of tree branches separate like a person was passing through them and then fall still as the floating lantern hit the edge of the tree line and quickly faded into the darkness.

After a few seconds of confusion and fear, he decided to get back to his car as soon as he could. Unfortunately, he would have to travel past the spot where the floating lantern had just disappeared right before his eyes. A chill came over him as he realized this, and he began peddling and shifting gears to gain as much speed as he could to put this place behind him. As afraid as he was, he still felt the urge to take a look as he approached that eerie point in the tree line. Against his better judgement, he peered to his left as he peddled by. He saw nothing unusual at first glance, but looking over his left shoulder as he passed, he saw something that shook him to the core. There, just behind the first layer of branches, were two sets of red eyes locked on him.

Railroad turned bike path in Kipton, Ohio. *From the author.*

The Guardian Angel of Lofton Henderson Bridge

Built in 1939 by American Bridge Company of New York, the Lofton Henderson Memorial Bridge, formerly known as the Twenty-First Street Bridge, carries four lanes of State Route 611 and a sidewalk over the Black River Ship Channel in Lorain, allowing an average of 14,310 vehicles to cross between the east and west sides of town every day. The complete lack of lattice and v-lacing in its truss members and bracing would have been almost unheard of among truss bridges of this size built during this time. This undoubtedly gave the bridge a unique look. Even today, this Lorain icon retains a rather striking appearance. The six-span, 1,704-foot-long, high-level, continuous-cantilever thru truss bridge has a main span of 400 feet and side spans of 200 to 300 feet long. The bridge is one of only eleven remaining examples of the design used for long, major crossings. For most of its life, it had been known as the Twenty-First Street Bridge, but in 1992 it was renamed for a genuine World War II hero from Lorain, Lofton Russell Henderson, who was killed at the Battle of Midway.

Born May 24, 1903, Henderson graduated from the United States Naval Academy in 1926. Before World War II, he served in China, at various Caribbean stations and on the aircraft carriers *Langley*, *Ranger* and *Saratoga*. He commanded Marine Scout Bombing Squadron 241 (VMSB-241) at the Battle of Midway. On June 4, 1942, as Japanese forces approached Midway Island in the Pacific Ocean, Major Henderson led sixteen Marine Corps SBD Dauntless dive bombers in a glide-bombing attack on the aircraft carrier *Hiryū*. His left wing burst into flames as he began his final approach.

Henderson continued the attack and perished as his plane dived toward the enemy carrier. For his selfless courage in battle, he was posthumously awarded the Navy Cross, the United States military's second-highest decoration awarded for valor in combat.

While the Lofton Henderson Memorial Bridge is named for a hardened combat veteran, the spirit that has been spotted there resembles a guardian angel of a fairer persuasion.

The high-level bridge has a second, equally important, purpose in the community. In addition to providing a way for vehicles and pedestrians to cross the Black River while allowing shipping traffic to traverse the waterway, it also provides local daredevils on two wheels a way to use the gift of gravity, along with the high arch of the bridge, to achieve speeds that could not be reached on a bicycle in any other place in the city. For decades, generations of these bicycle bandits have used this unique advantage to feel the wind on their faces as they never have before. That's just what a young man named Alan was doing in August 1982.

Making his way home on the east side of Lorain, Alan was looking forward to the bridge because he could get his bike up to speeds that would actually break the speed limit posted for cars on the bridge. Just before eleven o'clock that night, after the long climb up the western half of the bridge, Alan finally crested the peak of the arch and shifted his Schwinn ten-speed into neutral and let gravity take over.

He reached his maximum speed just as the bridge met the sidewalk on the east embankment. Visibility was very good, despite the hour, due to a series of streetlights that illuminated the sidewalk along Henderson Drive. That's when he noticed something on the sidewalk. Initially, he couldn't quite make out what it was he was seeing, but when he figured it out, he was sent instantly into a panic. It was a young, attractive woman who just seemed to appear out of nowhere. Tall and slim, she looked to be in her early twenties, with shoulder-length blond hair. She wore an open collar white shirt, blue jeans and white deck shoes. She was standing on the sidewalk, running one hand through her hair.

The sidewalk was narrow, and with a guardrail and a steep drop-off to the river on the left and two lanes of oncoming traffic on the right, Alan knew there was no way he could maneuver around her. He shouted to get her attention, yanking on both brake levers, hoping to somehow stop in time.

He was within twenty feet of her when she suddenly disappeared. Alan stopped the bike a few feet past where she'd been standing and looked around, but there was no trace of her. She would not have had enough time to step out into the street and cross to the other side. He would have been able to see her somewhere. If she had gone toward the river, he would have heard her crunching through the dry grass and weeds. She just vanished right before his eyes.

Puzzled, Alan slowly walked the bike farther down the sidewalk, trying to find the young woman. Then he saw something that gave him a chill. About ten yards beyond where she had been standing, there was a large chunk of concrete missing, leaving a hole all the way across the sidewalk. Alan realized immediately that if he had hit the hole at the speed he was traveling, he would have lost control of the bike and either been thrown down to the river or out toward the road and into oncoming traffic.

Whoever or whatever the vision was, she had very likely saved his life.

Gore Orphanage: Fact and Folklore

Of all the ghost stories in Lorain County, and likely in the state of Ohio for that matter, the legend of Gore Orphanage is certainly among the most famous. It is *the* ghost story for every teenager within a twenty-mile radius of the infamous road, who consider it almost a rite of passage to wander into those harrowing woods at night in search of the phantoms their older siblings warned them about. Beyond the curiosity of the local adolescents, the area has been the subject of countless books and newspaper articles over the decades. A search on YouTube will result in more than its fair share of videos posted by everyone from giggling teenagers to the most ardent ghost hunters. It even has its own Wikipedia page. There was a forgettable movie in its name released by Amazon in 2015, but unfortunately the name is the only thing the film has in common with the events that took place in Swift Hollow in the early twentieth century. But almost none of the nearby residents have use for any of this, for we all know the story. Well, at least some version of it.

I was just eleven years old when my older brother Rich told me the tale. It went something like this:

Deep in the isolation of Swift Hollow, there once stood an old mansion that was converted into an orphanage by a money-hungry tyrant named Gore. Sinister Mr. Gore used the children as slave labor in the surrounding fields to further increase his fortune while barely providing them with the necessities for survival. They slept five or six to a bed, were fed calves' lungs on the rare occasion they got to eat, and were forced to drink the very water they bathed in. The building itself was in shambles and provided little protection from the elements. The children were eventually reduced to catching and eating the rats that lived in the dilapidated structure with them just to survive. A life of misery was put to a grisly end one October night when a fire broke out on the first floor of the building. Possibly set intentionally, it trapped the children in their dorms on the levels above. In just minutes the entire structure was ablaze. Of the more than one hundred children forced to live in that terrible place, not one survived. It is said that if you are brave enough to enter those woods at night and stand at the remains of the foundation of the orphanage, you will be rewarded with the smell of smoke from a building that burned down a hundred years ago, and even worse, you'll hear the children's screams in the air as if the agony of their unimaginable demise would last throughout eternity. On the rarest of chances, you might happen upon some of the children on their way to eternally work Ol' Mr. Gore's fields.

This was pretty scary stuff, particularly for a young lad who spent his evenings listening to Art Bell and his *Coast to Coast* radio program on the paranormal. Since we happened to be in Rich's Ford Escort with my other brother Rob and his buddy, also named Rob, en route to Gore Orphanage when the newly licensed eldest brother shared this story, I was utterly terrified. The two Robs didn't seem to be all that impressed with the tale, but looking back I am certain that was just a tough-guy act.

The trip to get there was eerie enough that it set the tone for what was to come—down a dark, narrow, winding road that descends sharply into the valley, around a hairpin turn where the headlights lose the road for what seemed like an eternity, across the river on an old narrow bridge and then farther into the darkness where the trees seem to close in on you. There is a noticeable sad, heavy feeling in the air as you make your way down Gore Orphanage Road. Finally, you reach a spot on the side of the road just big enough to park a car—or to turn it around since no reasonable person would willingly get out of a vehicle in a place like this after dark. Of course, what is reasonable to a group of teenagers? We did the unthinkable and got out of the car and made our way to the trail opening. The fall of autumn leaves had rendered the path nearly undetectable, but after a brief search we located the opening and headed—in the dark—toward what had to be, in my eleven-year-old mind, the most terrifying place on earth.

We reached the foundation within minutes. It didn't look at all as I had expected. I imagined that it would be a large, flat slab of concrete in the shape of the original mansion, maybe with some charring from the fire.

Foundation ruins at Swift Hollow. *From the author.*

Foundation ruins at Swift Hollow. *From the author.*

Foundation ruins at Swift Hollow. *From the author.*

I hadn't taken into account how time and nature would work on the slab. Instead of the even, well-defined shape I had anticipated, what lay before us looked far less man-made. The foundation had broken up over time, pieces large and small were randomly strewn about. Years and years of freeze-thaw cycles broke the concrete and stone into various-sized pieces. Large chunks lifted into ramp-like structures as the ground beneath them shifted and reformed continuously over the last century. Smaller pieces had been moved around by both man and nature. Saplings had found homes in the gaps, growing large and spreading their root systems out and further distorting the landscape. What was left appeared to be more of an outcropping of stones in a forest landscape than something that had once supported an entire mansion. For a moment, as I took in the bizarre scene, I had entirely forgotten the reason we were there.

As the four of us wandered in random directions, looking but not really knowing for what, I tried to imagine where the rooms of the house had been. Was this where the kitchen was? Or was this some kind of family room or maybe a dining hall? As I thought more about the house, I began to think about the people inside the house. Then it hit me: I was standing in the spot of one of the most horrific events to have ever taken place. A hundred

Graves of Heman and Tryphenia Swift in Andress Cemetery. *From the author.*

people or more died in this very spot. Not just people, kids. A hundred kids died here—probably kids my age. My bewilderment at the landscape was instantly replaced with dread.

That was my first experience at Gore Orphanage. The truth about Swift Hollow is that there was a real tragedy that took place there, and the old mansion did burn down in 1923. Unfortunately for the story we grew up with, the mansion had nothing to do with Gore Orphanage.

In 1817 Joseph Swift, a successful farmer from Massachusetts and veteran of the War of 1812, purchased more than four hundred acres of woods in the valley surrounding the Vermilion River. A year later he married Elizabeth Root and began building a promising future in farming. He built a cabin on the property and began clearing the land. His family grew along with his farm, and he and Elizabeth eventually had six children.

Swift would spend the next twenty years clearing the land in preparation for his dream home, leading the neighboring farmers to refer to the property as "Swift's Folly." Construction began in 1840 and was finally completed two years later at an exorbitant cost of $15,000. The finished product was a true specimen, a stunning, single-story Greek revival mansion unlike anything in the area at that time. The home consisted of fourteen rooms with fifteen-foot ceilings, six fireplaces, servants' quarters and a magnificent veranda with large Greek pillars. Its many rooms were appointed with elaborate furnishings, ornate woodwork, marble columns and other lavish decorations, and the home was immediately considered one of the most fashionable in all of Ohio. Swift named his creation Rosedale and lived in the home with his wife and children for decades. The architecture of the mansion was so different that it was featured in a book published in 1936 titled *Early Homes of Ohio*, written by Ihna Frary. Frary wrote, "The broad recessed porch with its four Ionic columns…gives the house rare distinction." He said, "Architects from far and near were attracted by the unusual character of the house, but its remote location led ultimately to its (eventual) abandonment." If you would like an in-person visual of Rosedale's architecture, the Ritter Public Library in Vermilion is modelled after the mansion.

The years in the remarkable Rosedale were not always happy ones for the Swift family. First his five-year-old daughter, Tryphenia, died. Ten years later, his son Heman died at the age of twenty-four. Things only continued to get worse. Finally, after a poor investment in a railroad venture had depleted his fortune, Joseph Swift was forced to sell his beloved Rosedale to Nicholas Wilber in 1865.

Members of the Wilber family were said to be spiritualists engaging in spiritual rituals even before they purchased the mansion. It is due, at least in part, to this reputation that the property began to be thought of as haunted by locals. The Wilbers would reside in Rosedale for almost thirty-five years.

Tragedy struck the family in the winter of 1893. Between January 13 and 19, four of Nicholas and Harriet Wilber's grandchildren—children of their son Miller—died of diphtheria when an epidemic swept across Ohio. All four children—Jesse, age eleven; May, age nine; and twins Roy and Ruby, age two—were buried next to each other at nearby Maple Grove Cemetery. They did not die at the Swift Hollow mansion, but at their parents' home in Berlin, Ohio. The tragedy ramped up the spiritual activity of the family, which would host séances attempting to contact the lost children. The grief overwhelmed Harriet, and she eventually descended into madness. It is said that she refused to believe the children were dead, whispering to herself as if talking to the children and setting the dinner table with four extra place settings. Her condition continued to spiral until her passing on November 10, 1899.

Nicholas Wilber lived in the mansion until his death in February 1901, when the property was sold to the Sutton family. Nicholas's final resting place was beside his wife in Maple Grove Cemetery, with many

Swift Mansion in Rosedale. *From Alan Leiby.*

other members of the Wilber family, including their four grandchildren. Rosedale stood vacant for the next several years and became known as the Haunted House of Gore.

The Light of Hope Orphanage (also called the Orphanage of Light and Hope or the Light and Hope Missionary Society, depending on the source) was established on the property in 1902 by John A. Sprunger, a Mennonite evangelist who had previously operated a similar orphanage in Adams County, Indiana. While Joseph Swift's abandoned mansion still stood on this premises, it is unclear whether Sprunger used the building for his operation. Some sources show it being used as quarters for hired farm hands while others have said that it was a guest house, but most claim the house remained empty.

The majority of the buildings used for the orphanage were farther south. The property had separate dormitories for boys and girls by the river at the top of the hill, as well as a chapel, a schoolhouse, a buggy shed and a print shop for the Light and Hope publication. A 1910 United States census shows that there were 45 people living on the property, including 27 children, Katie and John Sprunger and 15 helpers and assistants. Sources show there could have been up to 125 children on the property at a single time and as many as 500 in total during the life of the orphanage.

Rumors about the orphanage, and about Sprunger himself, began spreading soon after its establishment. Stories of the mistreatment of the children circulated through the surrounding area, casting a dark shadow over the orphanage. A lack of schooling, clean water, proper meals and regular bathing, as well as the practice of severe beatings as punishment, were some of the stories that found sympathetic ears. The children contributed to the gossip, as many of them ran away from the orphanage and into town, begging not to be returned. They told people how Mr. Sprunger and the other farm overseers would mistreat and neglect them and how they were not given enough food or proper medical attention. They also claimed that they were sometimes rented out to other farmers in the area for labor. After these stories were printed in the local newspapers, an investigation was launched by the state in 1909. Investigators found many of the rumors to be true. Even though Mr. Sprunger admitted to some allegations against him, the state of Ohio had no laws or regulations pertaining to the operation of such institutions at that time, and little action could be taken against him.

John Sprunger died in 1911—two years after the investigation. In his absence, the orphanage suffered from financial troubles. Citing severe financial hardship, the orphanage officially closed its doors in 1916. Children were dispersed throughout the community or returned to relatives or guardians who could be found. The few who had nowhere else to go traveled back to Berne, Indiana, with Mrs. Sprunger. The mansion was once again abandoned, slowly losing its battle with the elements until finally succumbing to the flames of a fire that spurred a legend that would endure for nearly a century.

No one is sure how the fire was started, but early in December 1923 the once-grand Rosedale went up in flames and burned to the ground. The story was published on December 8, 1923, in Elyria's *Chronicle-Telegram*.

> *Only two spectral stone chimneys now stand on the site of the old haunted house that has been a mystery at Mill Hollow [sic] for many years. The colonial mansion burned to the ground in a midnight blaze. Neighbors, who heard mysterious noise around the place on stormy nights, swear that spirits were screaming in the trees at the height of the blaze. How the fire started is a mystery....The haunted house was the mecca for thousands of tourists. Names of visitors from all quarters of the globe adorned the dilapidated walls of the house.*

It has been well established that the mansion had been vacant for years by the time it burned down in 1923. The orphanage was in operation in the years prior, but they used several buildings farther down the river, and it's unclear if the old abandoned mansion was used at all during this time.

It's true that some of the children relayed tales of mistreatment, but even the worst of these don't add up to the slave-labor story we heard as kids. And none of them, or anyone else, perished in the fire. What has likely occurred is a conflation of two separate events that both happened in the early twentieth century: the burning of Swift Mansion and the Collinwood School fire in 1908.

The Collinwood School fire was a true disaster by any measure. As many as 172 students and 2 teachers were lost in the most horrific way imaginable. Many who couldn't be identified afterward are buried in a mass grave in Lake View Cemetery in Cleveland. When you take this event into account and combine it with a building associated with an orphanage that happens to be on a road called Gore, the story practically tells itself.

What about the people who smell burning wood when they go there? When you visit Swift Hollow in the daylight, the scene is a little more serene. You can see more of the houses in the area, with actual living people occupying them. It wouldn't be too much of a stretch to assume at least one of those nearby houses might have a fireplace or a wood burning stove. And of course, the most obvious time to visit such a notoriously haunted place would be on a dark October night—right about the time people would need to start heating their homes at night or maybe just enjoying the romantic glow emanating from their fireplaces.

And those screams? The Ohio Turnpike was completed in 1955, and it so happens that its route lies just south of the infamous Swift Hollow. The phenomenon known as "acoustic shadowing" is created when sound waves fail to propagate an area, such as a hollow, due to topographical obstructions that, along with the forests surrounding the area, can filter out much of the noise generated by the highway. What is left is the high-pitched whine of the tires of tractor trailers at highway speeds, which, with the aid of an active imagination and a really good ghost story, can indeed sound like a chorus of screams.

This is not to say that there isn't anything tragic about the place, and I'm not only speaking of the Wilbur children, who died during the diphtheria outbreak of 1893. Certainly, losing four children in six days would be devastating to any family, and by all accounts, the trauma shattered Harriet Wilbur. The stories of the family holding séances in an effort to contact their lost grandchildren could be true given they were already known to be spiritualists.

The tragedy I speak of is more contemporary and, sadly, ongoing. According to local law enforcement, an average of two or three people every year choose Swift Hollow as the place to intentionally end their lives. Perhaps they find its remote location a fitting scene, or maybe they are inspired by the legends that persist there. Maybe the Wilbers stirred up something supernatural with their séances, and whatever it is still remains attached to the area. The heavy feeling in the air I mentioned does exist to those who are sensitive to such things, and perhaps that has something to do with it. Regardless of their reasons, it is truly sobering to think of so many lives that are needlessly lost in one place. Whatever demons or spirits that exist there, they are palpable, and they affect each and every one of us in different ways.

THE WARDROBE

After his father lost his job when the York International plant in Elyria closed, seven-year-old Patrick, along with his parents, moved into his grandparents' house on Mechanic Street. Having grown up there, Patrick's father, Mike, had to swallow his pride by moving in with his elderly parents because that was exactly what his wife and son needed him to do. His parents had extra room, and his mother was ecstatic at the prospect of having her grandson around every day. The four-bedroom colonial was starting to show its age, especially on the second floor, where it seemed nothing had been touched in decades.

Young Patrick still got to have his own room, taking his Uncle Dan's old room at the top of the stairs. Still filled with the furnishings Dan had used more than thirty years ago, the only thing Patrick cared about was whether it had ample floor space for his Thomas the Tank Engine set, and it did. It even had the perfect place to store his other favorite toys—an old, dark wardrobe standing in the corner, though it did have a musty smell to it.

After the first week, everyone seemed to fall into a routine. Mike spent the majority of his time looking for work, while his wife, Sarah, helped around the house when she wasn't working part-time at the Hills Department Store in Elyria. Patrick spent his time helping his grandpa in the garden and engineering the perfect rail system in his room when he wasn't being doted on by his grandmother.

One day while the family was sitting at the table for breakfast, Patrick asked his dad about the time Uncle Dan had accidently tripped coming out of his room and nearly fell down the stairs.

"Where did you hear about that?" Mike asked curiously, knowing that no one in the family had heard from Dan in more than three years.

"Roscoe told me about it. He said that Uncle Dan tried to tell everyone that he was pushed, but no one believed him."

Mike had his coffee mug halfway to his face but stopped and set it back down on the table after hearing the name Roscoe. He looked over at his son with grave concern. "Who did you say told you that?"

"Roscoe. He lives in the wardrobe in my room." Patrick was looking down at his cereal and didn't pick up on his father's distress, but it was certainly there.

"He must be awfully small to live in a wardrobe," Mike said, prying.

"He is. He's smaller than me, but he's old and kind of smelly. He's really nice to me and he knows lots of stuff."

Mike looked across the table at his mother, who sat there in shock as her eyes began to well up. After a few seconds of silence, he reached beside him to grab his wife's hand before he spoke up. "I've got a great idea, bud. Why don't we see if Grandma can take you to the park after breakfast? I hear they finally got those new swings up, and it's supposed to be a beautiful day today."

Sarah didn't know what was going through Mike's mind at that moment, but she knew him well enough to recognize when he was shielding Patrick from something. But from what?

Twenty minutes later, as his mother backed out of the driveway with Patrick strapped in the back seat, Mike walked to the garage and went inside. Two minutes later he emerged, pushing a furniture dolly with one hand and carrying an eight-pound sledgehammer in the other. He leaned the sledgehammer against the house next to the back door and carried the dolly inside and up the stairs.

"Mike, what's going on?" Sarah asked as she followed him up to the second floor.

"My brother, Dan" he said, not breaking stride. "All his life, he talked about his imaginary friend. He blamed every poor decision he ever made on that thing. Never took responsibility for any of the terrible things he's done," he went on as he entered Patrick's room and wheeled the dolly directly over to the wardrobe.

"I don't understand. Dan hasn't been around in years. What does he have to do with what Patrick said?"

Mike pulled the wardrobe doors open and emptied the contents onto the bed. Then, moving in a calm and deliberate manner, he closed the cabinet's doors and began pulling it away from the wall.

"Dan was troubled. No one could ever figure out why. Doctor after doctor, they all came up empty. They put him on some pills, and he'd just get worse," he continued, not even acknowledging Sarah had said anything at all. "No matter what we tried, nothing ever helped."

"He told us all the time that it wasn't his fault. He told us 'he' was making him do it, but of course we didn't believe him." Mike lifted the wardrobe up with the dolly and started to make his way slowly down the stairs, listing out loud all the awful things his older brother had done when they were kids. Reaching the first floor, he carefully wheeled through the house and out the back door. Finally reaching a spot in the middle of the yard, he set the wardrobe down and pulled the dolly free, wheeling it back toward the house.

"Dan started using drugs when he was thirteen years old," he said, picking up the sledgehammer. "In and out of rehab all through high school until he dropped out in eleventh grade. He never cared about what that did to Mom. He never cared about anything but himself and his imaginary friend." With that he took a swing, sending the sledge crashing into the wardrobe, and he continued to swing. Blow after blow, he didn't stop until the large piece of furniture had been reduced to a pile of scrap wood. He dropped the hammer and walked back into the garage—this time returning with a gas can and a box of matches. He started pouring the gasoline all over the battered pile of wood.

Sarah, who had stood there listening to Mike the entire time, still could not connect the dots. "What does all this have to do with Patrick?" she asked again as he set the can down.

Mike pulled a match from the box and struck it, then looked directly into Sarah's face for the first time since breakfast. "It was Roscoe, the little old man who lived in the wardrobe. We didn't believe him, but that's what he always told us. That's who drove Dan insane."

Restless Rest Area

As you travel west down State Route 2 just before you reach Erie County, you will find the last rest area for the next 60 miles on this road. Known to the Ohio Department of Transportation as Rest Area 3-44, this stop, as with most rest areas on our freeway system, is in an isolated area between more populated areas. Surrounded by a scenic wooded lot with elevated views of the Vermilion River, it's a great place for travelers to stretch their legs after a few hours behind the wheel. The beautiful setting may be the reason why a woman chose this location to end her life in the early 1980s.

The following was our experience at the rest area in 2016. We happened to be on one of our ghost tours when we pulled into the rest area for a restroom break one October night. As our group filed into the building, a short, thickset man in his mid-fifties with a mop in his hand walked over to us and asked about the bus. I described the various tours and services we offer and that we were on our way to Gore Orphanage. His face lit up at the mention of the ghost tours.

"You know this rest area is haunted, don't you?" he said. He introduced himself as Jeff Hastings and told us that he had been the night caretaker for almost nine years. He said he had personally witnessed some pretty strange things in his time working there.

It was Jeff's belief that everything started when the body of an unidentified woman was found slumped over one of the picnic tables just a few yards from the rest area building. Having died from what looked to be a self-

Rest area in Vermilion, Ohio. *From the author.*

inflicted gunshot to the head, it was ruled a suicide by the local authorities. She was dressed in a powder blue two-piece workout suit and running shoes. On the bench next to her was a nearly empty purse with no money or identification. It contained only a Polaroid photo of a young girl sitting on a plaid couch, a cigarette case with seven Winston cigarettes and a 35mm film container holding a handful of unknown pills. The .38 caliber revolver was found at her feet with a single spent shell casing in the cylinder. She did not match the description of any missing persons in the surrounding areas, and eventually the effort to identify the body was abandoned. It was assumed that she was likely homeless, or maybe a prostitute from some other part of the country—possibly robbed and left behind at the rest area by some unknown traveler or truck driver. With little physical evidence to go on, the case went cold and still remains unsolved.

Jeff claimed that on more than one occasion he had seen legs—without a torso—wearing blue pants, walking past the building's windows as he mopped the floors inside. Sometimes he could hear talking in the trees near the overlook, but no one was ever there. He also spoke of the time when a male traveler came to him looking for help because he had heard a woman crying in the women's restroom. When he walked to the doorway, Jeff said he could hear her too. He opened the door slightly and called out to her

Rest area in Vermilion, Ohio. *From the author.*

through the space between the door and its frame, asking if everything was OK. She didn't seem to hear him, so he repeated his question louder. Again, there was no answer, so he slowly pulled the door open and stepped into the room. Nobody was there.

On another occasion, a woman traveling alone stopped for a late-night break. As she walked from her car, she noticed someone with long hair sitting at one of the picnic tables facing away from the restroom building. While inside, she heard a loud sound from outside the building, which she later described as a "single bang." Upon exiting the building, she saw that the long-haired person at the table was gone, and when she detected a strong odor of gunpowder lingering in the air, she rushed to her car and drove off, concerned for her own safety. She placed a call to local law enforcement the following morning to report the incident. They sent a patrol car out to investigate the area. Nothing out of the ordinary was found.

During my conversation with Jeff, he revealed a few details about his personal life, such as being raised on an Indian reservation in Oklahoma. He described himself as something of a gypsy, moving from place to place in his earlier years. He mentioned that his time living in Ohio and working at the rest area was the longest he had stayed in one place since he left Oklahoma when he was sixteen years old. He also brought up that he would like to get back to Oklahoma someday to visit family that still lived there.

We parted ways with a handshake and an agreement that I would find him again for further details about the alleged hauntings. In my mind, a new stop for the ghost tours that also offered public restrooms and vending machines sounded ideal.

I decided to do a little more research of my own on the rest area, which turned up more than the one suicide at that location. In fact, with the most recent incident taking place in 2010, it happens more than you would like to know. Most of the time the stories are kept out of the local papers in an effort to deflect unwanted attention from the area, so the names can be difficult to come by.

I returned to the rest area a couple weeks later with my wife, Judy, and Donna, the paranormal investigator we hired to guide the ghost tours, hoping to get a little insight on the location. We ran into two workers that day, but unfortunately neither of them were Jeff. As we spoke to these other men, things started to get a little strange. While they were both aware that there had been some suicides on the grounds and they each had heard rumors of weird sightings, neither of the men had any recollection of ever working with anyone named Jeff. Furthermore, they told us that there wasn't a position of night caretaker, and no one was permanently stationed at any one rest area. The position required them to service multiple sites each day, and they were usually only in one place for an hour or two.

"Did this Jeff give you a last name?" asked one of the men.

"Hastings. He said his name was Jeff Hastings," my wife replied.

"Did you say Jeff Hastings?" the other worker said in disbelief. "I know of a Jeff Hastings, but I'm pretty sure you didn't talk with him two weeks ago. Nine years back, on my first week working here, we found a man dead in his car right over there. Shot himself. His name was Jeff Hastings."

A Tale of Two Theaters

Largely due to the demand for industrial labor, the city of Lorain was growing rapidly in the 1920s. Founded on the mouth of the Black River with access to the Great Lakes shipping lanes and the eventual railroads in the area, it was a prime location to host an industrial boom. Because of the companies that took root in the city earlier in the century—like the American Ship Building Company on the river and the United States Steel Corporation's steel mill on the south side—people from all over the world made the journey to Lorain. This is how Lorain became the "International City," as it is known today. Throughout the early 1920s, the population continued to rise, the economy remained vigorous and things were looking up for the budding metropolis. That all came to a halt on June 28, 1924.

Much like it is today, Lorain was a tough, blue-collar town filled with tough, blue-collar people, which is why it is no surprise that, despite a poor weather forecast, all the downtown shops and businesses were bustling with patrons on this Saturday afternoon. Living on the south shore of Lake Erie has its advantages, but it also means that wild swings in the weather are a part of everyday life. But June 28 would be a day like no other—Mother Nature was about to show off her magnificent and terrifying power.

After striking the northern edge of Sandusky to the west, a massive tornado moved out over the lake and headed east before making landfall on the beach in Lorain's Lakeview Park shortly after five o'clock in the evening. The storm cut a three-mile-wide path through the city, damaging or destroying more than one thousand homes in a thirty-five-block stretch, along with every business in the downtown area. An estimated two hundred cars were buried in rubble or thrown into the lake by what is now estimated to have been an F4 tornado. By the time the wind stopped blowing, seventy-two residents of Lorain had lost their lives to what is still ranked as the fourth-deadliest tornado in the northern United States.

Among the leveled buildings was the popular State Theatre, located on the east side of Broadway, just north of Fourth Street. Patrons had filled the theater to catch a matinee show, but nearly two-thirds had made the fortuitous decision to leave during intermission due to the brewing storm outside. For many of those who had chosen to remain, it would be a fatal decision. The theater reportedly held its own against the storm when it finally hit, but it was doomed by the collapse of the adjacent Wickens Furniture building. The upper floors of the seven-story building landed on the roof of the theater, but the structure held long enough for many of the remaining patrons to flee into the streets. It wasn't long before the added weight proved to be too much for the smaller building, and the roof finally gave way, smashing the balcony and those still on it. In all, fifteen people perished in the State Theatre that day—the most killed in a single building during a tornado in Ohio. Almost all the victims had been seated on the balcony.

Tornado devastation in Lorain, 1924. *From Alan Leiby*.

Tornado devastation in Lorain, 1924. *From Alan Leiby.*

Tornado devastation in Lorain, 1924. *From Alan Leiby.*

Tornado devastation in Lorain, 1924. *From Alan Leiby*.

As part of the massive initiative to rebuild downtown Lorain in the years following the devastating storm, the 1,720-seat Lorain Palace Theatre opened in 1928 to replace the destroyed State Theatre. Money was no object in the design of the new theater. It featured a Wurlitzer pipe organ that rose from below the stage; an ornate and gracefully domed ceiling in the main auditorium that was highlighted by a custom-made, three-quarter-ton Yugoslavian crystal chandelier; and two Peerless Projection machines that would allow film to run continuously without a break for rewinding. It was groundbreaking from the very start, as it became the first theater in Ohio to show a talking motion picture, screening the "talky" *Something Always Happens*, starring Neil Hamilton and Esther Ralston, on the theater's opening night.

While most theaters share similar characteristics in design and layout, there was one fundamental distinction between the Palace Theatre and the old State Theatre. Given that most of the fifteen souls lost in the storm in the previous theater had been a result of the collapse of the balcony, it was feared that the city's residents, with the memory of such a catastrophic disaster, would be hesitant to frequent a similarly designed structure. Faced with the potential of lost revenue, it was decided to avoid the feature in the new structure, making the Lorain Palace Theatre the largest single-floor motion picture theater in Ohio at the time of construction. That decision, along with all the new innovations, paid off. From opening night until the

Lorain Palace Theatre. *From the author.*

building of the Midway Mall in neighboring Elyria in the mid-1960s, the Lorain Palace Theatre and the rest of downtown Lorain enjoyed the fruits of being the entertainment and shopping hub of much of the county.

Of the many thousands of guests to have enjoyed the performances at the Palace over the decades, there seems to be at least one man who is believed to be more of a permanent resident than a patron. Described as tall and dressed in outdated clothing, he has made physical appearances at various points within the building and has quite possibly made his presence known in other ways since the 1950s. Nearly thirty sightings of the man have been reported by people of all ages from different eras, yet the experiences were always similar. He is known as the man in the brown coat.

Typically, sightings of the man occur between shows when the theater is quiet. At first, witnesses assumed that he was just a stagehand milling around the stage, carrying out his duties. Since there is always work to be done around the stage, many of the people who saw him didn't give him a second thought. He's most commonly seen descending the short set of stairs on the left side of the stage, on the theater floor and making his way to the emergency exit door on the east wall. On these occasions, he does not acknowledge the presence of the onlookers in the theater, appearing determined to reach his destination. As the sightings continued, witnesses who took notice of his unusual 1920s-style brown overcoat began to pay closer attention to his movements. Some have claimed to watch as he seemed to vanish through the door instead of opening it to make his exit. Others have noted the lack of sound as he moves—as if he is floating instead of walking. A larger man crossing an old wooden stage and down some stairs in an empty theater—in any type of shoes—would surely make at least some noise.

Alice from Elyria, a lifelong resident of Lorain County, said,

> *I remember seeing the man in the brown coat when I was a little girl. I grew up in Lorain and my mother would take me to see movies there at the Palace during the summers. We were usually early for the show because I had my favorite seats, and I wanted to make sure no one else got to them before we did. On that day, my mother had gone into the lady's room, so I started down the aisle with my popcorn in hand. The movie screen was down over the stage like always, but I noticed something in front of it—off to the left side. I just stopped right there, trying to get a better look, I guess. Normally, I wouldn't give much thought to a man in a public place like that, but it was the long, brown coat he was wearing that seemed out of place, looking back at it. It was late-June, and it must have been in the 80s that day. He also had a hat on, and in those days, it was considered inappropriate to wear a hat indoors. A strange sight, indeed. I didn't feel frightened—he was too far away for that. It just seemed odd. His head didn't move, and I don't remember seeing his legs at all. He started to move toward the far end of the stage, his brown coat contrasting against the giant white movie screen. And right as he got to the edge of the stage, he just disappeared. Just like that. The whole thing lasted about twenty seconds.*

Alice's experience was similar to most of the other witness accounts, but not all have been as innocuous. One man recalled his experience a little differently. He had also grown up in Lorain, and he, too, spent his summer afternoons enjoying matinees at the Palace. As an adult, his job as a civil engineer had taken him to several places both overseas and in the United States before he finally settled in Colorado. On a trip home to visit family members who still lived in Lorain County, he was feeling nostalgic as he drove down Broadway and decided to stop in the Palace to relive some childhood memories. After getting permission to walk around, he entered the empty theater and took a seat in the very back of the middle section. His eyes moved left to right as he scanned the beautiful Italian Renaissance décor—his gaze stopping at the platform for one of the two emergency exits on the west wall. There stood a tall man in a long brown overcoat

Lorain Palace Theatre. *From the author.*

and a hat, whose silent stare gave the visitor the impression that he was not welcome. He sat for a few seconds fixed on the imposing figure until, menacingly, the man in the brown coat started to make his way toward him. If the message was vague initially, it was now clear as a bell. He immediately sprang from his seat and dashed out of the theater. Once back in the marble lobby—heart still racing—he began to tell a staff member about what just occurred. Recognizing the description of the figure, the staff member looked at him and said, "Ah, I see you have met our ghost."

Given his 1920s attire, it is speculated that the spirit that lingers in and around the theater was perhaps one of the unlucky souls on that balcony of the State Theatre that came crashing down in 1924—now sentenced to wander the theater for an eternity in search of his loved ones. Others have theorized that he was perhaps a performer from another time whose deep love for theater has prevented him from moving on in the afterlife. Still others believe that he was a former employee of either the Palace or maybe even the State Theatre—a stagehand or caretaker still carrying out his duties.

The man in the brown coat has certainly made an impression, but the strange happenings at the old theater haven't been limited to his appearances. There have been many employees throughout the years who have refused to be alone in the dressing rooms behind the stage for various reasons—unexplained voices whispering from the adjacent room, sudden temperature drops or just a creepy feeling that would come over them. Faint sounds of old music that sound like a phonograph emanating from under the stage have been reported by workers multiple times. On several occasions, the fifteen-hundred-pound crystal chandelier has randomly and mysteriously turned on—completely illuminating the auditorium during performances and movies. Sometimes this will last for just a few seconds but other times for as long as thirty minutes. Theater technicians have been unsuccessful in finding the cause of this, as were the electrical engineers brought in by management for further investigation. Though it has been several years since this last occurred, the staff knows that it is a possibility at any time. Perhaps the man in the brown coat is expressing his displeasure with the current movie or stage performance. Maybe he is still stuck in that fateful day in 1924 and is using the lights of the chandelier to warn the theatergoers of impending disaster. Perhaps he has simply maintained a sense of humor and delights in the annoyance of the crowd.

The Lorain Palace Theatre is truly a magnificent place—particularly for those of us who have so many memories of it. A fixture of the urban hub in this Rust Belt town, generations have enjoyed the Palace not only for its musical and theatrical performances, but for weddings, graduation ceremonies and other civic events. Contemporary buildings just don't have the same gravitas, never mind the historic significance, of the old theater. You almost get a sense of being transported to another place—another time. Indeed, with its long history and early-twentieth-century décor, stepping into the Lorain Palace Theater can make one feel as though they have stepped back into the heyday of a once-vibrant community. And for others like the man in the brown coat, perhaps that community is still there.

DAREDEVIL OF BARRES ROAD

Older residents of North Ridgeville can remember back to the late 1960s, when a tragic but predictable motorcycle accident on Barres Road took the life of a young, foolhardy man one summer night. The single-lane road was relatively remote back then, cutting through a field from east to west, and the quarter-mile stretch of asphalt was often used as a drag strip by the area's young men on motorbikes. These daredevils would come off Case Road from the west and open their throttles wide, shifting gears as quickly and as smoothly as they could to get their bikes screaming to maximum speed before reaching Otten Road to the west. For one man, the exhilaration of the night air whipping his face at such speeds could only be achieved while on his 1965 Harley Davidson Panhead Electra Glide, and he chased that feeling every chance he could. Little did he know that this night would be the last time he'd ever know that feeling.

Just like hundreds of times before, he downshifted his transmission into first gear and pulled his clutch, applying his brakes steadily to bring his bike to a crawl as he slowly took the left onto Barres. As soon as his bike was upright, he released the clutch and rolled his throttle all the way back, forcing his Panhead to roar violently to life. He was pushing forty miles per hour in mere seconds as that coveted adrenaline rush coursed through his body. He knew he could reach sixty miles per hour before reaching Otten, but each night he tried to get there a little sooner. On this night, he would not make it there at all.

About halfway down the narrow stretch of road, something went wrong. Perhaps it was a mechanical failure of some kind, or maybe an animal lept from the darkness into his path. Since there were no witnesses, no one could say for sure what happened. Whatever the reason, it was over in seconds. His bike veered left off the pavement and directly into one of the large maple trees that lined the north edge of the road, mangling the Harley and killing the rider instantly. It is said that the impact was so violent that his head was separated from his body and found in tall grass some thirty yards from the tree.

This section of the road is now closed, having been determined by the city to be unsafe for traffic due to a deteriorating culvert that carries the road over a drainage ditch. That minor inconvenience hasn't been enough to deter the innumerable bands of thrill-seekers determined to find the tree that took the young man's head more than fifty years ago. They have all heard the stories, and they want to see for themselves if they are true.

One legend says that if you stand before the tree at a certain time and wait, it won't be long before you see a single headlight closing in on you at an alarming speed. This would be your cue to flee the scene, as no one who has made it that far has ever seemed to muster the courage to stick around long enough to find out what happens next. Most have never made it to that point, instead compelled to vacate the scene after hearing the roar of a motorcycle in the distance even before finding the right tree.

There are several residents of homes around the corner on Otten Road who have seen enough inexplicable occurrences that they are convinced something from the spirit world is lurking in the darkness of that field. One resident has had several sightings of the same ghostly figures of an old woman and child dressed in old-fashioned clothing. She initially thought the image was the result of sleep deprivation until a neighbor told her the previous owners of her home decided to move after experiencing the same figures in the house. In another home on the same street, a family's three-year-old has spoken of wanting to play with the kids in the field—kids no one else has ever seen—and occasionally about the nice old man he talks to through the window on the back of the house. Other kids from the newer Meadow Lakes development built adjacent to Barres Road have said that during a summer evening bike ride, all five in the group heard screaming coming from the direction of the field where the man's head was found.

The most disturbing story of all, and perhaps the most revealing, is of a young woman driving home from work late one Friday night. Making her way from her job at the Pizza Hut on the corner of Abbe Road and

Barres Road in North Ridgeville. *From the author.*

Broad Street in Elyria to her home in Avon, she was driving down Otten as a shortcut to Stoney Ridge Road. As she approached the intersection to make a right onto Barres, an elderly man in ragged clothing appeared from behind an obstruction on the right side of the road and stepped out into her lane, forcing her to swerve left toward the opposite side of the road. After coming to a stop, she rushed out of the car to check on the old man. She searched franticly in the darkness for several minutes, but he was nowhere to be found. Shaken, the girl got back into her car and drove off, thinking about finding a new route home from work.

Is it possible that whatever ran that poor guy off the road and into the tree back in the '60s had tried to claim yet another young soul?

There Goes the *Calico Jack*

While it was the Eighteenth Amendment that established Prohibition, it was the Volstead Act—passed by Congress on October 28, 1919—that enforced the law. This act clarified that "beer, wine, or other intoxicating malt or vinous liquors" was any beverage that was more than .5 percent alcohol by volume. The legislation also stated that owning any item designed to manufacture alcohol was illegal, and it set specific fines and jail sentences for violating Prohibition. Across Lake Erie to the north, Canada had its own version of Prohibition, but its legislation never included a ban on the manufacturing of liquor for export. This gave rise to a massively profitable and extremely dangerous business of illegally transporting alcoholic beverages across international borders, known as rum-running. As a result, Canadian distillers would be the source of 80 percent of liquor smuggled into the United States during the 1920s.

North of Kelleys Island, just inside Canadian waters, lies a tiny patch of land known as Middle Island. This island is the southernmost point of land in Canada, providing a natural migratory corridor for birds and other animals. It has also seen human migrations—mainly from the United States northward in the nineteenth century, including escaped slaves, prisoners of war and army deserters from the Civil War, seeking asylum in mainland Ontario. During Prohibition, however, the island was a way station for alcohol en route to the south shore of Lake Erie—from Detroit to Erie, Pennsylvania.

Gangster Joe Roscoe acquired part of the island and built a seven-bedroom "clubhouse" that became the center of rum-running activity. The hotel offered electricity, fireplaces and a large screened-in porch with views of the lake. Allegedly one of the hotel's most notorious guests was Al Capone, who was rumored to have stashed his lost fortune somewhere in the walls. The contraband whiskey, brandy and beer would be brought to the island legally under Canadian law, where it then would be loaded onto "contact boats," which were small, local boats that usually operated under the guise of fishing vessels. The smaller, quicker boats could more easily outrun Coast Guard ships and could dock in any small river or eddy and transfer their cargo to a waiting truck for a tremendous profit. These huge rewards meant the rum-runners were willing to take big risks. They ran without lights at night and in fog, risking life and limb. Often, the shores were littered with bottles from a rum-runner who sank after hitting a sandbar or a reef in the dark. The most daring and successful of these rum-runners was a man who went by many aliases but was most commonly known as Oren Isaac.

Isaac was a crafty and skilled smuggler, deploying tactics that most men could never dream of. Educated, charismatic and fluent in four languages, he could usually charm his way out of any jam he found himself in. He always seemed to be two steps ahead of his pursuers—the United States Coast Guard. Oren was famous for keeping cans of used engine oil handy to pour on his hot exhaust manifolds in case a smoke screen was needed to escape. When it came to "hauling the mail," there was no one quite like Oren Isaac.

As skilled as he was, Isaac owed much of his success to the *Calico Jack*, the twenty-six-foot modified dart boat he named for John Rackham, the early eighteenth-century English pirate captain. Its deep "V" shape and planing hull were perfect for cutting through the choppy waters of Lake Erie at high speed. Widely considered to be the fastest contact boat on the lake at that time, his vessel could easily reach speeds of more than fifty miles per hour. Even fully loaded with as much as seventy-five cases of liquor, the *Calico Jack* could speed across the lake at night, outrunning any Coast Guard vessel.

This is not to say that Isaac had never experienced any close calls. He once watched as the Coast Guard seized the *Calico Jack* while he had been ashore. It was not uncommon for rum-runners' ships to be sold at auction, and the *Calico Jack* was awarded to the highest bidder when its day came. That bidder was an incognito Oren Isaac.

Eventually, Isaac's run as the greatest rum-runner on Lake Erie would come to an end, and true to form, it would happen in one of the most swashbuckling ways ever witnessed on the Great Lakes. Having been turned in by an informant while porting in a cove of the Black River, Isaac opened his throttle and daringly raced his way through a three-ship blockade at the river's mouth. The *Calico Jack* made into open waters, but only after enduring a barrage of gunfire from the three Coast Guard vessels. The gunfire ruptured the vessel's fuel cell and ignited the gasoline spilling onto the deck. The speed of the boat forced the wind to feed oxygen to the flames, and soon the entire hull was ablaze and illuminating the horizon. The vessel made it nearly a mile from where the Black River empties into the lake before the *Calico Jack*, and its flamboyant captain, were overtaken by the fire and disappeared beneath the surface of the water.

It is said that Oren Isaac is still out there making his runs in the dead of night. After the sun has slipped behind the horizon, people on sailing vessels who are returning to port on the Black River can sometimes hear the sound of a small vessel motor pass them, but they can observe no sign of the boat nor a wake in the water. They then say, "There goes the *Calico Jack*."

Lady of Garden Avenue

Linda could never sleep until he got home. Her husband, Duane, was never one to work a nine-to-five job, so the late nights were just a way of life for the young couple. After the baby went down for the night, she would pick up a book and read until he got home. This meant she read more than she slept most days. Not that she minded—reading was a passion she had inherited from her mother, and this had become a comfortable routine for her and Duane since they moved into the apartment a few months ago.

The Garden Street apartment was small, but with just the two of them and the baby, they really didn't need that much space anyway. The price was certainly right, and the landlord, one-hundred-year-old Mrs. McGee, was an absolutely delightful woman. She loved to boast about how she had raised ten children of her own in that old house before sectioning it off into four separate apartments when the last one left the nest. For the most part, the place was exactly what they needed.

Duane was a large man by any standard, standing at six foot four and tipping the scale at just shy of four hundred pounds, but he carried himself like a man of half that weight. Quick-witted and charismatic, he had the agility of a cat while possessing the strength of a dump truck. These attributes added up to him fitting his current job like a tailored suit. For the last two years he had been the go-to muscle behind Lorain's largest underground bookie organization, run by Ralph Ramirez.

If you lived in Lorain in the '70s and '80s, you may be familiar with Ralph's store R & R Sales in the now-demolished Oakwood Plaza on Pearl

Garden Avenue and West Eighteenth in Lorain. *From the author.*

Avenue. The store sold bingo supplies to the local churches and little trinkets and candy to the neighborhood kids who stopped in after catching a matinee at the Lorain Twin Cinemas. The place was actually able to turn a small profit most years, but its true purpose was really just to serve as a front for the gambling outfit that was run out of the back. That's where Ralph made his real money.

I'd recommend picking up a copy of the book *Luck Was My Lady* if you have ever been interested in learning more about the darker side of the city's history. Despite it being listed as fiction, Ralph wrote the book as sort of a tell-all while serving out his prison sentence. It reads like Lorain's version of the Martin Scorcese film *Casino*, and it's fascinating. The names were all changed, of course, but if you lived in Lorain around that time, I'm sure you'll recognize some of the characters.

Duane was always home late, but late turned into three o'clock in the morning when Ralph ran his "Las Vegas Nights" at the shop. Entering the apartment put you in the center of the main hallway. At the end of the hall to the right was the kitchen, the bathroom directly in front of you and the bedrooms down the hall to the left. Linda was in bed reading her book as usual when she heard Duane enter the apartment and close the door behind him. After a brief pause, she heard him call out, "Linda?" in a low voice.

"I'm in here," she replied from the bedroom. There was about four seconds of silence before the sound of his large frame came rumbling down the hall. He burst through the bedroom door and dove straight onto the bed, burying his face in a pillow and thoroughly baffling Linda. "What the hell are you doing?" she said, startled.

"I just saw a woman go into the kitchen." He looked up from the pillow and saw the confused expression on her face. "In a white nightgown. I thought it was you." He had expected her reply to come from the kitchen, not the bedroom, and it sent him into a near panic.

Linda erupted in laughter. "You think you saw a ghost, don't you?"

Duane was a legitimately tough guy—as tough as anyone she had ever known—and seeing him act like this was quite amusing to her. "Aren't you a little big for ghost stories?" she asked, still laughing. He was embarrassed, but Linda was likely the only person in the world who could get away with deriving so much amusement at his expense.

A couple weeks later, Linda was again in bed with her book. It was Casino Night, so it would be another couple of hours before Duane would be home. She was nearly finished with the Louis L'Amour novel she had borrowed from her mother, *Cherokee Trail*, and was already wondering which book she'd read next. She leaned back on some extra pillows at the headboard of the bed, reading from the light coming through the window from a lamppost in the alley behind the old house. The bed was situated in the far corner of the small room with the door to the hallway in the opposite corner of the adjacent wall.

She was about halfway down the page when she became aware of the presence of someone else in the room. In her peripheral vision, she could see a dark-haired woman in a long, white gown standing at the foot of the bed. Frozen with fear, Linda just stared at her book, too terrified to look up. Not knowing what to do, scenarios raced through her mind for what seemed like an eternity. Finally, she couldn't ignore it any longer, and she worked up the courage to look at the figure. When she lifted her eyes over the book, the ghostly figure had already started moving back through the bedroom door, and the only thing Linda managed to see was the tail end of the woman's gown as it slipped into the hallway and out of sight.

What she initially suspected to be a burglar, she now recognized as the same entity that had spooked her husband two weeks earlier. She didn't feel threatened, but alone with an infant in the home, she didn't feel very comfortable either. She placed the book on the table next to the bed and slowly got up and walked to the door. Flipping the switch on, the hallway

Garden Avenue in Lorain. *From the author.*

instantly flooded with light, revealing nothing out of the ordinary. Doing the same in the rest of the rooms in the small apartment, she decided to wait for Duane in the living room.

When he finally got home, she told him what happened. "That's it, we're moving," was his response before she could even finish her story. True to his word, they did three days later. Duane was as tough as they come—known to be willing to take on any man, physically or otherwise. Any man. This was something different—something he wanted no part of.

SPIRITS OF THE *SPIRIT OF '76*

On the southern end of Lorain County, at the intersection of State Routes 58 and 18, is the village of Wellington—a place with as rich of a history as almost any other small town in the country. Incorporated as a village in 1855, Wellington soon developed into the "Cheese Empire of the Nation," a powerhouse in the American cheese industry due, in large part, to the sprawling dairy farms in the surrounding area. Much of its growth, and the construction of its beautiful Victorian homes, was partially due to the relatively short train ride from the largest city of the region, Cleveland, and the industrial moguls, who sought quiet locations for their summer homes. The present town hall was built in 1855 and features an unusual combination of Byzantine, Greek, Gothic and Spanish influences. This building included the largest opera house between Cleveland and Columbus and was host to many of the most popular shows of its day. It is said that the village was named after William Welling, a local resident, while others contend that the name is derived from the title of the Duke of Wellington. Regardless of where the name originated, many of our nation's largest historic moments had roots in this unassuming village.

While the neighboring town to the north gets much of the recognition in the abolition movement in the mid-1800s, one of the most important pre–Civil War episodes on the subject took place in Wellington. In 1858, the former American House Hotel was the site of the famous Oberlin-Wellington Rescue. A group of men, both white and black and many from Oberlin, swarmed the hotel to rescue runaway slave John Price. He was being held by a U.S. Marshal and his men and was waiting for a train that would return him to his master in Maysville, Kentucky.

The abolitionists transported Price out of town and, through Underground Railroad channels, helped deliver him to freedom in Canada. Afterward, thirty-seven men were indicted for their actions, but only two—Simeon M. Bushnell and Charles Henry Langston—were tried in federal court for interfering with the marshal, who was enforcing the abominable Fugitive Slave Law. After Langston delivered an impassioned speech about the sinister nature of slavery and discrimination, the sympathetic judge gave them light sentences. The events and trial garnered attention across the country.

Wellington's most famous resident was Archibald M. Willard, a nineteenth-century painter. After moving to Wellington from Bedford, Ohio, in 1855, Willard became an apprentice to Edward S. Tripp, who employed Archibald to paint carriages and furniture. This experience provided Willard with his first formal training as an artist. Once, after not receiving payment for a job where he painted apples on the side of a carriage for a local fruit grower, Willard snuck into the barn where the carriage was kept after dark and painted over artwork, effectively repossessing his work for nonpayment.

In 1863 Willard left Wellington to enlist in the Eighty-Sixth Ohio Volunteer Infantry to fight in the Civil War. He started to draw pictures of

Archibald Willard's *Spirit of '76*. *From the author.*

what he saw during the war and, in partnership with photographer James F. Ryder, began to sell reproductions of his work. The two men continued their business relationship for years, until Willard decided to go to New York after the war's end to study art with Joseph Oriel Eaton.

In 1875 Willard moved to Cleveland, Ohio, where he set up a studio. During this time, he became known for his work painting three murals—the *Spirit of Electricity*, the *Spirit of Telegraphy* and the *Spirit of the Mail*—in the main hall of the Fayette County courthouse in Washington Court House, Ohio. Willard also painted his most famous work in Cleveland, a painting featuring two Revolutionary War drummers and a fifer, known as the *Spirit of '76*. Originally called *Yankee Doodle*, the painting was exhibited and widely seen at the Centennial Exposition in Philadelphia, Pennsylvania, in 1876. Willard drew his inspiration for the painting after he saw a holiday parade pass through the town square in Wellington in 1875. The original is displayed in Abbot Hall in Marblehead, Massachusetts. Several later variations painted by Willard have been exhibited around the country, including a large rendition that hangs in the United States Department of State.

Willard used his father, Samuel Willard, as a model for the middle character of the painting. Hugh Mosher was the model for the fifer, and the smaller boy was Henry Devereaux. Though the painting was not well received by critics, it was hugely popular with most Americans as it stirred a sense of patriotism within them. Ryder produced many images of the work to sell to the public, and Willard painted a number of different versions of it for the remainder of his life. Willard died in 1918 and is buried at the Greenwood Cemetery on the southern edge of Wellington.

The Spirit of '76 Museum, located in Wellington, is dedicated to Willard and the history of Wellington and southern Lorain County. Many of Willard's works are displayed there, including wall murals taken out of a local home before its demolition, painted portraits of both his mother and father and a variation of the *Spirit of '76*, along with the original drum and fife used as models in the painting. Founded in 1968, the museum also displays more than four thousand artifacts of historical value—from Native American artifacts to military weapons and period clothing and even an x-ray machine used by a local shoe store to get a visual of the fit of customers' shoes from the 1930s to the 1950s. The building itself is something of a relic, having originally been built in 1870 as one of the first warehouses for the cheese industry that was booming in Wellington at that time.

Spirit of '76 Museum in Wellington. *From the author.*

As with most older buildings, the museum can project an eerie aura, particularly if you happen to be wandering around its interior alone. Even people who have volunteered there for years still experience that eerie feeling. One member of the museum's board has even admitted to not wanting to be in the building in the dark. He quickens his pace as he starts on the third floor, turning the lights out as he makes his way down and ends up in a near-sprint by the time he reaches the street level. Even for visitors, being among so many artifacts can leave them wondering if the previous owners had been so attached to them that they have stayed with them, even after death.

That could explain some of the strange things that have been experienced at the museum. At different times, several women wearing dresses have spoken about sudden bursts of cold air moving past their legs while on the second floor. The southeast corner of that level is known as the "touch corner" because so many people have felt the sensation of being touched while standing alone there. One young woman, while in the library, thought nothing of her boyfriend standing so close to her back that she could feel his breath on her neck. She got the attention of everyone in the room when she let out a scream upon looking up and seeing that he was standing on the opposite side of the room, and no one was behind her at all

A young man named Wyatt, grandson to Cindy—one of the museum's volunteers—has spent countless hours in the museum while his grandmother tended to her duties and has had more than his fair share of odd experiences. Long after losing interest in the historic items in the museum, Wyatt had to find a way to keep himself busy. It doesn't take much for a boy with a ten-year-old's imagination to find entertainment in such a place. Wyatt believes he has made a "friend" at the museum, even if no one else can see him. Often, Wyatt would feel his "friend" sharing his seat as he sat in the library. Once, after Halloween, the generous young man offered to share his trick-or-treat candy with his new buddy. He sat a box with a single Milk Dud in the middle of the table, where he sat with several others. Everyone thought it was a kind, though misguided, gesture. That is until, to the shock of everyone, the candy suddenly and ever so slightly moved, seemingly on its own. Then there was the sound of an impact followed by the rattle of the lone Milk Dud in the box.

One evening, Wyatt and his "friend" were playing with a tennis ball, mischievously rolling it across the glass top of a display case on the second floor. Standing at one end of the long, rectangular case, he rolled the ball toward the opposite end. As it neared the edge on the other side, the ball would come to a stop, reverse course and return to his waiting hand. Realistically, a slightly pitched floor in a 150-year-old building certainly wouldn't be unheard of, and gravity could account for Wyatt's partner in this game. That is what was going through his grandmother's mind as she watched from the other side of the room. After several moments of repeating this trick, Wyatt rolled the ball once again. As it had each time before, the ball came to a stop just as it reached the last few inches of glass before the edge. This time, instead of changing direction and coming back to him as it had been, the ball remained stationary. His grandmother watched as Wyatt calmly walked down to the other end of the case and picked up the ball. As he moved past his grandmother on his way out of the room, she stopped him and asked why the ball had just stopped and not rolled back to him. "He was done playing," was Wyatt's response.

There is another possible explanation for the strange happenings in the old building. The murder-suicide that took place in the building to the north may be the reason an unseen presence is felt at the museum.

In November 1890, Samuel L. Sage was the sixty-three-year-old owner of a grocery store operating on the ground floor of the Crosier building, abutting the cheese warehouse and eventual museum next door. For years, Sage had operated the grocery store with his wife, until her passing from rheumatism just a few months before. His trusted employee, David Hoke, was also in his sixties and had previously worked for decades in the carriage business in the employ of Edward Tripp, just as Archibold Willard had. Both men were highly regarded in the community.

A law man in town, Marshal Williams, had observed some unusual behavior by Hoke, opening the grocery at irregular times—sometimes as early as half past five in the morning. After noticing this, Williams observed that the same female customer was shopping at that strange time of day and leaving "with well-filled baskets." Williams decided to notify Sage of the possibility that something inappropriate, maybe even criminal, was going on at his establishment. Initially, Sage did not believe the allegations, but after confronting Hoke directly, the clerk confessed.

The woman in question turned out to be Emma Gardner, the twenty-eight-year-old wife of a railroad worker and a relatively new resident in Wellington. Mrs. Gardner was attractive and had light hair and blue eyes. The marshal implied that she had been observed using something a little more salacious than cash in exchange for her groceries. She was charged with theft, but she claimed that she assumed the purchases were being charged to her husband's account. She was last seen boarding a southbound train a week later, skipping town and her trial.

The two men, along with the marshal, agreed Hoke could avoid arrest by making financial restitution. In an unusual arrangement, Sage consented to allow Hoke to work off the debt in his grocery store. It would prove to be a fatal decision.

The following Monday, Marshal Williams was on patrol when he heard shots from inside Sage's grocery store. He rushed through the door to find Samuel Sage bleeding on the floor from a bullet wound on his temple. David Hoke was in the back room, also with a fatal gunshot wound to the head. It was evident that Mr. Hoke had come to believe that the humiliation of his actions was more than he could bear, and he had decided to take his innocent employer out with him. Hoke died within minutes on the scene, and Sage was carried to a nearby house, where he died three hours later.

To emphasize the strong reputation Mr. Hoke had in the community, the *Wellington Enterprise* wrote in his obituary, "There probably was no more prompt man in Ohio to meet his obligations. His credit was gold-tinged, and although he was possessed of some weak points of character, he had many virtues which would not come amiss for the average person to observe." It is rather odd that probable sexual misconduct and most assuredly murdering one of the village's more prominent citizens would be considered a few weak points of character.

It is unclear what started this violent act, but it is believed that such abrupt endings can leave spirits to wander the area in confusion. It has been speculated by many that the spirit of Mr. Sage or Mr. Hoke, or perhaps both, are the cause of the unexplained events in the museum, having met their violent demise mere feet from its door.

There is one other set of circumstances that could play a role in the museum's mysterious happenings. There was another tragedy that befell yet another prominent member of the community, again just feet away from the museum's door.

In 1925, eighty-four-year-old Dr. Edwin R. Holiday was crossing Oberlin road, now more commonly called OH-58. Known around town as simply "Doc," the retired surgeon was still practicing in Wellington as a veterinarian and was likely on his way to tend to his duties. A Civil War veteran, Holiday had enlisted in F Company, Third Ohio Volunteer Calvary in 1881, at the age of seventeen. He took part in one of the war's bloodiest battles in Shiloh, Tennessee, and by the end of the war had earned the title of sergeant. After medical school, he spent the remaining years of his life serving the people of Wellington and nearby Clarksville in Huron County.

Perhaps his advanced age had impaired his judgement, or maybe he was just in a hurry that day. Doc Holiday entered the street and stepped into the path of an oncoming trolley that operated in town. The doctor was killed instantly.

It was a tragic end to a full and prosperous life, and a real loss to the community, to be sure. What made this event so terribly ironic was that twenty-two years prior, in 1902, Doc's twenty-year-old son, Malcom, had lost his life at almost the same spot. Malcom was crushed by the rear wheels of the trolley car he had been riding. There had been some speculation that Malcom may have been pushed from the vehicle, but there was never any evidence to support the claims, and the event was ruled an accident.

In addition to the two coincidentally tragic events that took place right in front of the cheese warehouse that would eventually become the Spirit of '76 Museum, among the thousands of artifacts on display, there is a section of track that was taken from the road during a repaving project years after the trolley service ended.

If you ever find yourself in Wellington with a day to kill, think of stopping in the Spirit of '76 Museum to enjoy a whirlwind trip back in time. And while you are there, maybe you can figure out who Wyatt's invisible friend really is.

Ghost Train at Cottesbrooke Curve

The interurban was a type of electric railway with streetcar-like, self-propelled railcars that ran within and between cities and towns. They were prevalent in North America between 1900 and 1925 and were used primarily for passenger travel between cities and their surrounding suburban and rural communities. The interurban was a valuable cultural institution. Most roads were still unpaved in the early nineteenth century, and transportation was mostly done by horse-drawn carriages and carts. The interurban provided vital transportation links between the city and countryside. By 1930 most interurbans were gone, including those that operated in Lorain County, and many of the lines were replaced with bus service. Oliver Jensen, author of *American Heritage History of Railroads in America*, commented that "the automobile doomed the interurban whose private tax paying tracks could never compete with the highways that a generous government provided for the motorist."

On the night of July 16, 1903, E.L. Gavin of Oberlin was killed in a trolley wreck on the Cottesbrooke curve, a section of a road now known as Oberlin-Elyria Road, where State Route 301 splits off to the south. Two cars on the Cleveland and Southwestern electric line came together in a horrific head-on collision near the Cottesbrooke farm two miles southwest of the city. The cars telescoped—the underframe of one vehicle overrode that of another and smashed through the second vehicle's body—but somehow managed to stay on the track. The term "telescope" is derived from the resulting appearance of the two vehicle bodies. The body of one vehicle may appear to be inside the other like the tubes of a collapsible telescope—the body sides, roof and underframe of the latter vehicle being forced apart from each other. A surviving passenger said that he was sitting directly behind the motorman and could look over his shoulder. He said the other car could not be seen because of the trees lining the curve, and he was not aware of any danger until the motorman suddenly leaned forward and attempted to stop his car. The next instant, he caught a glimpse of the other car emerging from the bridge and in another moment, they had collided. In addition to the death of Mr. Garin, somewhere between twenty and fifty people were injured in the mangled wreck. One other person supposedly died later from injuries sustained in the crash, but a name for that person could not be found. It was later determined that the wreck occurred because of human error: there was a misunderstanding of orders at the switching station that allowed an eastbound train onto the same track the westbound car was traveling

For many years after, trolley workers passing through the area where the accident occurred reported seeing a shadowy figure standing in the middle of the track, only to disappear when the headlight shined on it. While nearing the curve and bridge at a good speed, one motorman said he was startled to see a shadowy figure standing in the middle of the track just a few feet from the bridge. The fear of hitting a pedestrian always lingered in the mind of the motorman, so he pulled back the throttle and blew the whistle to warn the walker of his approach. The darkened figure moved over to the side of the track, and the car was able to decelerate to a crawl by the time it rounded the curve. The headlight illuminated a clear stretch of shining rails and ties ahead. The form had vanished before the light had a chance to catch up to it.

On one particularly snowy evening, two brakemen had been sent out from the powerhouse to keep the tracks clear of snow on the Cottesbrooke curve. While sweeping the tracks, they heard the sound of a rapidly approaching railcar. Both stepped back from the track to await the passing of the car.

Both men could hear the train approach. Nearer and nearer it came, they would later claim, until its deafening noise was upon them, but they saw no train. No headlight broke the gloom of the whirling snow, and no car flashed by them, they said, until the sound of a tremendous crash silenced it.

The cry of a human in mortal anguish followed the crash. Both men stood stupefied, listening as all fell silent as death. Standing in disbelief and fear, the men gazed briefly at one another before dropping their brooms and leaping over the tracks, running full speed back to the powerhouse.

The Caretaker

What is now known as Valley of the Eagles Golf Club, the Spring Valley Country Club opened in 1926 and served Elyria and greater Lorain County as one of the premier event locations for decades. In addition to its PGA-rated golf course, the facility housed an event center and multiple lounges and bars. During its peak years, the operation required a sizable staff, and many through the years have reported having an encounter with the spirit of what is believed to be a former caretaker. Never a threatening or intimidating presence, the man seemed to be observing or watching over the grounds and the people within with an occasional flash of his unique sense of humor.

Several members of the staff and some of the patrons experienced the most common occurrence over multiple decades. The front door to the main lounge opened and closed, seemingly on its own, and was immediately followed by the sound of heavy boots climbing the nearby stairs to the second floor. Once there, the sounds always stopped, as if whatever it was had become weightless and floated away.

The kitchen staff often found themselves to be the target of the caretaker's sense of humor. Cooks would find their utensils in odd locations. Other kitchen staff would have the walk-in freezer door close behind them when they entered the unit, but it would otherwise stay open if no one was inside. This happened with such regularity that the employees started to prop the door open with a heavy object. Even that didn't always have the desired effect, as the door would still find a way to close itself, pushing the heavy object out of the way.

Once, a waitress walked into the kitchen to find two of her coworkers standing in front of a pile of shattered glass with their jaws dropped and faces pale. Dropping a glass in a restaurant happens daily, so she found their petrified reactions to be somewhat strange. She asked about the broken glass, and they just looked at each other in disbelief—each wondering if the other would be able to explain what they had just witnessed. One of them finally spoke up, telling the waitress that he had watched the glass lift itself out of the drying rack and throw itself onto the floor while the other employee stood, nodding without saying a word.

The lounge—known as the Red Bar due to the color's dominance in the décor—seemed to be a favorite room for the spirit, as it had made itself visible on several occasions. One patron reported arriving at the lounge just after it opened. He settled on a seat at the bar, two stools away from the only other patron there, who was oddly underdressed in overalls. The bartender entered the room from the back, and she asked the man if he would like to order a drink. He responded that the other man was there before him and that she should take his order first. When he turned to point him out, there was nobody there. Another time, a bartender noticed someone standing silently at the far end of the bar. It had been particularly slow that night, so she thought it was odd that she didn't notice him walking in. She looked down to grab a menu and started walking in his direction to greet him. The bartender had only made it halfway there when she saw the man slowly fade into transparency and just vanish.

It was the responsibility of the last employee of the night to go around the building and turn off all the lights before leaving. They would start at one specific area and work their way around the building, coming full-circle to the room where they started. On several occasions, as an employee would get back to the starting point, they would find the lights had all been turned on again.

One woman who would often be the last to leave the club had told some coworkers about her feeling of being watched as she walked alone to her car. She always wanted to look back to see if anyone was actually there but felt too afraid to do it. One night, after locking the door, she was walking across the parking lot and finally decided to take a look over her shoulder as she reached the car. Sure enough, there in a second-floor window above the main entrance stood a man dressed like a farmer staring down at her.

Then there was the time in the early 80s when Spring Valley hosted an event featuring psychics. One of the guest speakers was a man named T. Albert Thomas, known at the time for his abilities in the field. At some point during his visit, he entered the Red Bar and declared, without any knowledge of the activity that had been experienced there, that this lounge would never enjoy long-term success. He went on to explain his reasoning—he believed the color of the room attracted the wrong kind of spirits, and eventually that would cause people to avoid the space altogether.

Saying Goodbye

Nine-year-old Madalia woke up early like she did almost every day. Sunday mornings were always a busy time at her house, and sleeping late was never an option, as she was expected to help her mother with the kitchen duties. Discipline was a constant in her family, but she didn't mind, especially on Sundays. In fact, Sundays were her favorite day of the week because that's when grandpa came to visit.

Papa, as she called him, was a large and gregarious man. To her he was a gentle giant, but he was the kind of man who would square his wide shoulders and look you directly in the eye with a broad smile across his face as his over-sized and callused hand firmly gripped yours, conveying his warm yet commanding presence. He had been a foreman in the steel mill for almost thirty years, and the men who worked under him looked up to him both figuratively and literally. Even in his older years, he maintained his towering posture and steady stride, and he still wore his heavy work boots well into retirement—almost as a symbol of pride for his blue-collar roots. He was rock solid and well-respected, and he absolutely adored his granddaughter.

Ever since Madalia could remember, her Thirty-Second Street home was the gathering place for all her relatives in Lorain's south side, and there were plenty. Her father's younger sister, her Aunt Rosie, with Uncle Miguel and her cousins, Juan, Carlo and Gabriela, would always be the last to arrive even though they had the shortest distance to travel, living right around the corner on Seneca. With their arrival, a total of sixteen people would gather every Sunday morning for breakfast before the group headed off to

East Thirty-Second Street and Seneca Avenue in Lorain. *From the author.*

service at Sacred Heart Chapel on Peal Avenue. This January day would be no different, despite the three inches of fresh snow that fell overnight. After freshening up in the bathroom, she headed downstairs to help with preparations. Papa was always the first to arrive, and she wanted to be the first to greet him at the door.

Madalia was a bright young girl and earned excellent grades at Lowell Elementary. Later in life, she went on to become a third-grade teacher at Lowell Elementary before finishing her career in California. She was a quick study, and her diligence and independence at such a young age made her parents and her Papa very proud. They were a close family, to be sure, but her special connection with Papa was something beyond that, and those few minutes that she would get him all to herself before the rest of the family arrived meant the world to her. She made it a point to have all her chores done, so when she heard the thumping of those heavy boots making their way across the wooden front porch to the door, there would be nothing to encroach on her cherished time with Papa.

As she finished setting the table, she looked up at the clock on the dining room wall above the buffet. Papa was usually there by now. Maybe the snow had slowed him down, she thought to herself. It wasn't like him to be late for anything. Ever. He was the kind of man who made it a priority to be punctual as a show of respect to those who expected him to be somewhere at a certain time, and he expected the same respect from others. Deep down she suspected something might be wrong, but she wouldn't allow her mind to wander down that road. It was the snow, she tried to convince herself, and she went into the kitchen to retrieve the pitchers of milk and water for the guests.

A few minutes later she set the last pitcher on the far end of the table. With her responsibilities for the morning now complete, she slowly spun herself around and faced the front door, listening intently for any indication of Papa's arrival—boots on the porch, a car door closing, his voice, anything. She stood quietly focused on the door for several minutes—the only sound she was aware of was her own beating heart. Why wasn't he there yet?

The silence was broken by a long ring from the telephone hanging on the wall in the kitchen. It seemed unusually loud to Madalia, and it startled her out of her trance. Her body jerked slightly as her head snapped in the direction of the obnoxious sound, taking her focus briefly from the still door. She listened as her mom moved across the kitchen floor, and as the phone was belching out a second alarm, she silenced it by picking up the handset.

East Thirty-Second Street in Lorain. *From the author.*

"Hola" she heard her mother say in her usual cheerful voice. Madalia's attention drifted back to the door. Any minute now.

Just then, she thought she heard something faint. Thump. She thought she heard it again. Thump. Yes, it's him, she thought, he's here! Thump. Still faint, she was sure it was the sound of her Papa's work boots on the wooden porch. Just as she was about to make a dash for the door, her mother called out to her. "Madalia," she said in a voice trembling. She turned to see her mother standing in the doorway between the kitchen and dining room. "Madalia, baby. Come here."

Madalia wanted to run to the door to greet her Papa, but she could tell by her mother's pained expression that something was terribly wrong. Concerned, she started toward the kitchen. Her mother leaned down and put her hands on her shoulders. "I have some very bad news, sweetie. Papa passed away in his sleep last night. He's gone."

Confused, Madalia held her gaze down toward the floor briefly before looking up into her mother's eyes. She had to be mistaken. "Momma, I just heard him outside," she explained in a panicked voice. Delivering this sort of news to a child is enough to break any mother's heart, and Mrs. Rodriguez's tears began to roll down her face.

"Uncle Rey found him in his bed this morning," she let out in a broken voice, trying to hold her emotions in check for her daughter's sake. "I'm so sorry, baby. He's gone."

Madalia still didn't understand why her mother would be saying this to her. She knew he was on the porch, and any second, Papa would be swinging the front door open. Hoping to alleviate her mother's anguish, she turned around and headed back through the dining room and into the living room. With no sign of the door opening, she made her way over to the large window adjacent to the door and pulled the curtain to the side. She had an uneasy feeling as she peered out the window, scanning the porch from left to right, hoping to see the large familiar figure. Her heart sank when she didn't find him there. She heard him—heard his boots on the porch just as she always did when he arrived—she was sure of it. With that familiar sound still playing in her head, her eyes lowered to the wooden floor of the porch. There in the newly fallen snow, she saw something that confused her even more. A single set of tracks on the porch halfway to the door, where they just simply ended.

Other Legends from Around the County

Amherst

Oak Point Road

South of Route 2 on Oak Point Road, across from Beaver Creek Park, is a field that is said to be haunted. In the late nineteenth century, long before the highway was built, a local man murdered his wife and supposedly buried her body somewhere in that field. In the months before her death, she had openly complained about how unhappy she was with her life. She had even gone as far as telling neighbors that she hated her husband, and she wanted to leave him in the dead of night and start a new life far from there. Little did she know that she was building a way out for her eventual murderer.

When the disappeared, no one was surprised. The police questioned the husband, but they had no reason to doubt him when he said that his wife had finally delivered on her promise. With her history of threats to leave him and no other obvious signs of foul play, the police were satisfied with the story, and there was no further investigation.

It wasn't until decades later that the man confessed to the murder on his deathbed. He said he had buried his wife in the field on Oak Point Road. There was a brief search but given the amount of time that had passed and the enormous size of the field, there was little hope of recovering a body, and the search was quickly abandoned. If the man was telling the truth in the moments just before his own death, then the remains of his murdered wife are still buried somewhere in that field.

It is said that in the early-morning mist you can see the shape of a woman wandering around in the field—perhaps in search of that new life away from her husband that she had dreamed of.

Old House on Cleveland Street

A young family relocated to Amherst after the father took a job in the area. After a brief search, they found what they thought would be the perfect home for the three of them. The realtor had disclosed to them that the previous owner had passed away of natural causes in the home, but they were not deterred. It was an older home, but it was close to his work and Amherst seemed like a great place to raise a family.

Almost immediately after moving into the house, the young couple's three-year-old daughter started talking about the ghost that lived in their new house. Initially the parents were not concerned because their daughter had already displayed a very active imagination. Given that Halloween had recently passed and she had a Halloween-themed picture book that she loved to read, they just assumed that all this talk of ghosts was just her imagination being fueled by the book. They thought it would be a phase that would eventually pass—especially with the other holidays just around the corner.

To their surprise, however, the holiday season came and went, and the little girl's reports of the ghost persisted. She would tell her parents that the ghost was in her playhouse in the basement, on the stairs or standing in the corner. She never seemed to be afraid of it and actually considered him to be her friend, so the parents decided to let it play out, still thinking her imagination would eventually move on to other things.

They remained convinced of this until a couple months later on a dark and rainy morning in March. The little girl's father was getting her ready to go to daycare when she told him that the ghost was on the back deck. She went on to explain that today was the ghost's birthday, and she wanted to sing him "Happy Birthday." Again, he mostly disregarded what she was saying about the ghost, as she made them sing "Happy Birthday" to Mickey Mouse, her Barbie doll and a stuffed dog named Louie in the past. Being a good dad, he humored his little girl and they sang and wished the ghost a happy birthday before loading into the car and going on with their day.

Later that day he started to think about what the realtor had told them about the previous owner. Out of pure curiosity, he decided to look up the obituary of the man who had died in the house. At first, nothing struck him as out of the ordinary as he read through the article. Suddenly, when he got to the part about the man's history, his jaw dropped.

Today was in fact his birthday.

Avon

Cork and Barrel Wine Bar

Formally the Vintage Café, this building is one of the original structures in Avon and at one time served as the community's doctor's office and hospital. According to the owners, an employee standing in the kitchen had a conversation with what they thought was another person in the next room, only to find out that there was no one there. The front door regularly locks on its own, and one of the cooks has witnessed a pot slowly slide nine inches across a stainless-steel table.

Unidentified Business

There is a business that wishes to remain anonymous that experiences paranormal activity on a regular basis, much of which is caught by the security cameras.

One example occurred when the owner came in one morning to open the shop. As he walked into the back room, he found a glass coffee pot smashed on the floor. He later questioned every employee who had worked the previous day, but none of them claimed to know anything about it. Unconvinced, the business owner decided to check the security footage. Sure enough, sometime during the night when the building was unoccupied, he saw the coffee pot slowly elevate over the counter, turn sideways and move across the room before suddenly dropping to the floor with a loud crash—all without any sign of anyone around.

This footage can be seen on the Scarlet Transportation & Adventure Tours Facebook page. Take a look and see what you think.

Avon Lake

Avon Lake Movie Theater

The theater is said to be haunted by a projectionist, who allegedly committed suicide. Employees of the Mona Lisa Eco Salon and Spa that now occupies the building have reportedly heard strange sounds coming from the former projection rooms that are now used for storage. Most say that there is a cold, dead feeling in the air and some even refuse to go up there. A former employee of another business in the building claimed that she was cleaning after hours one night when she heard the strange noises, though she thought she was in the building alone. She decided to investigate. She climbed the stairs and opened the door to see a strange, semi-transparent man with his back turned to her, then fled the building and never returned to her job.

Elyria

Allied Waste

On Butternut Ridge Road on the south end of town is the Allied Waste facility, also known as Republic Waste Management. Employees have reported seeing dark, shadowy figures in and around the building. Doors have opened and closed without explanation, and lights have turned on and off. Footsteps have been heard upstairs when no one else was in the building. Crashing sounds and bumping noises have also been heard.

Employees have dubbed the ghost "Frank."

Elyria High School

It is rumored that the tunnels beneath the school were haunted, although there is no explanation as to why. Paranormal activity has been reported in the old Washington building, and a large hot spot has been felt in the auditorium. Employees at the school have experienced strange things during the day. Mysterious music and talking can be heard when the school is supposed to be empty, but the source is never found. Security guards have reported seeing the image of a person running down the hallway, and it has been said this has been captured on the school's camera monitors at night, though the footage has never been revealed to the public. The guards checked all of the doors and windows and found them all locked and no one else in the building.

East Carlisle Elementary School

Just south of the Elyria city limits on Grafton Road sits the old East Carlisle Elementary School. It was once part of the Midview School District, but it was replaced when the new elementary schools were built on the Midview campus. The building now sits abandoned.

There was an old janitor named Ed who worked there when the school was in operation. Ed passed away sometime in the early 1980s, and the district hired a replacement for him. The new janitor had issues with keys disappearing from his keyring and finding tools in places he would never leave them. Once, he had the door slam behind him in his workshop, leaving him trapped inside for more than two hours before someone was able to let him out. Some of the other faculty took to saying, "Thanks Ed," when a cranky old radiator that had stopped working would somehow start putting out heat again before the new janitor arrived to fix it.

Possibly the hardest thing to explain was the time the principal came to the school on a Saturday morning to set up for an event scheduled that afternoon. He unlocked the door and entered the building to find the floor still wet from a recent mopping, even though he was the first and only person there.

Highway 113 Pond

The pond sits on the property of the Elyria Community Church of the Nazarene at the end of Clemons Avenue and is visible from State Route 113 most of the year. Motorists driving past this man-made pond have reported seeing a glowing human-shaped figure floating above the middle of the pond, walking in mid-air and often staring at the passing cars.

Spruce Street

Witnesses have reported seeing a dark, legless, ghostly figure wearing a black cape hovering along Spruce Street in the pre-dawn hours. The specter is most commonly sighted in the one hundred block of Spruce Street near the intersection of Lake Avenue.

Grafton

A man's body was found near the former Baltimore and Ohio railroad just west of town in the early 1910s. It was originally thought that the man died after being struck by one of the passing trains, but medical examiners found that he was already dead when the train struck him. Law enforcement believed that he had been murdered, and his body was placed on the tracks to cover up the crime. He was from Elyria and had a reputation as a heavy drinker. It was also known that he had recently come into a relatively large sum of money, which was not found on his mangled corpse, giving motive to the crime. With little evidence, no suspect was ever apprehended.

In the decades since, Grafton locals have seen their fair share of hobos and drifters along the tracks, but there has been one mysterious figure who has been spotted and doesn't appeared to have aged in fifty years. He is recognizable by his dated clothes and disheveled appearance, and he seems to be intoxicated at all times. The sheriff's department and police have both received calls about his presence, but he vanishes before they can respond. He never speaks to others nor does he even acknowledge their presence. He just drunkenly wanders along the tracks, searching for something unknown to anyone but himself.

LORAIN

Duane Building

The Duane Building is one of the oldest commercial structures and one of the most recognizable buildings in downtown Lorain. Built in 1906, it is one of the few buildings still standing that predates the 1924 tornado. Housing ten apartments, commercial space and a warehouse, the building served Lorain for decades. In February 2002, after being vacant for some time, a fire destroyed portions of the upper floors of the Duane Building, but the sandstone block foundation, exterior walls and steel beams inside the structure were relatively undamaged. It was believed that squatters accidentally ignited the blaze on the third floor while trying to stay warm. Following the $2 million rebuilding project, the Duane Building reopened in October 2004. The original ten apartments and two storefronts were redesigned to include nineteen apartments, six commercial spaces and a restaurant.

Former residents have smelled the scent of flowers where a flower shop was once located. Others have smelled cigar smoke in an area that was used as a smoking room in the early part of the last century. A mysterious woman has been spotted several times inside the building, silently walking the corridors. Several witnesses saw figures in the shape of men standing in the windows of the third floor during the fire, but when firefighters rushed in there was no one there.

G Street Park

Legend has it that a railroad spike that was removed from a hole unlocked a gate that allowed spirits into the park. The figure of a ghostly woman has been seen near the park on Grant Street. Anguished screams are heard throughout the night during certain points of the lunar cycle.

Old Southview High School

People have reported hearing basketballs bouncing and people talking in the first-floor gym when no one else was in the building. Dark figures with glowing eyes have been seen staring out of the windows after dark. A very tall, dark figure has also been spotted in the parking lot and disappears when approached. Sounds of a wooden baseball bat hitting a ball have been heard from the empty baseball field.

Old Whittier Junior High School

Teachers have claimed to have seen the tall figure of a well-dressed black man roaming the halls of the building when they have stayed late after school. They have also claimed to have heard locker doors slamming shut, the voices of children and chairs being scooted across the floors of empty classrooms, weird knocking sounds coming from the roof and the feeling of being watched.

North Ridgeville

The Diederich Farm

Across the road from the house of the Robber Ghost is a pair of houses that sit on the property that was once the Diederich Farm. Crop rotation—the practice of growing a series of different types of crops in the same area in sequenced seasons to help reduce soil erosion and increase soil fertility and crop yield—was commonly practiced by the farmers in the area, and the Diederich Farm followed suit. The small farm produced enough to sustain the Diederichs by filling the produce stand they operated at the front of the property on U.S. 20. The property once spanned forty-seven acres from Case Road on the east to where the Ohio Turnpike now lies on the west, but it eventually succumbed to commercial and residential developers over the years—much of it being purchased to build Lake Ridge Academy.

The adult grandchildren of Josephine, who was among the last of the family to occupy one of the houses of the farm, were charged with preparing the houses for sale. Debbie, daughter of Rita, who grew up on the property, was in the "small" house one day, preparing it to be put on the market. She was alone, but she was constantly distracted by the feeling of another presence in the room with her. She thought it could be her great-grandfather, who was killed on the road directly in front of the home after accidently stepping in front of a passing car. Or maybe it was her grandmother, Josephine—the same Josephine who had called the radio station about the strange events happening across the street at the Robber Ghost house—who even after her passing came to visit from time to time. The family would often play card

Diederich's "little" house. *From the author.*

games in the kitchen of the old home, and occasionally they would hear the sound of the door of the back porch open and close. That was followed by the door from the porch into the kitchen, where they were seated around the table, also opening and closing. After a few seconds, a third door—one leading from the kitchen into the next room—would open and close as well. Debbie remembered her father, Erv, would say, "Hi, Mom," to his mother-in-law, as they were all convinced it was her making her way through the home. Debbie had been very close to Josephine, and she felt somewhat saddened to think of selling her home.

Debbie's task for this day was to pull up some old carpet in the living room. As she pushed the carpet into rolls after separating it from its gripper strips, Debbie was surprised to find some old newspapers that had been hiding between the carpet and the floor. Curious, she knelt to the floor to pick up one of the old publications and began to scan over it. She found herself amused initially, comparing the headlines to today's news headlines and noting how the sensationalism hasn't seemed to change that much. She could not determine the timeframe of the printing by the articles, so she looked up at the top of the page to find the date. When she found it, she immediately dropped the paper and shot up to her feet. She knew the date, as it was one of the worst days of her life.

That newspaper she had just had in her hands was dated February 15, 2003, the very day her beloved Grandmother Josephine had passed away.

Sheffield Lake

The Senator's House

A troubling tale took place in one of the large, beautiful homes built along Lake Erie. The three-story home was once known as the Senator's House, and the owner, Dr. Ernesto Punsalan, a fifty-four-year-old general surgeon, lived on the first floor and basement level with his wife and their adult son, Ricky. The second floor was rented as a one-bedroom apartment, while the third floor, originally built as a ballroom, was used by the Punsalans as a music room.

Ricky had mental health issues, and he claimed that evil spirits in the home had continuously tormented him for years. The tenants of the second-floor apartment, a firefighter named Jeff and his wife, Sue, could attest to the spirits' existence in the mansion, though they never felt tormented by them. Among other strange events, the couple would sometimes hear music coming from the third floor when they knew they were the only ones in the home at the time.

Dr. Punsalan's daughter, Elizabeth, was an Olympic ice dancer and had won the U.S. national ice dancing championship in Detroit with her partner and husband, Jerod Swallow, in early January. They were the only American ice dancers who qualified for the Winter Games. The family had been planning a trip to Norway to attend the 1994 Olympics.

On February 4, around nine o'clock at night, Theresa Punsalan called the police after finding her husband, Ernesto, lying in their bedroom with two stab wounds in the chest. Dr. Punsalan was pronounced dead on arrival at St. Joseph Hospital in Lorain.

Having just been released from a mental institution earlier that day, Ricky immediately became the primary suspect and was arrested. He would confess to stabbing his father twice with a seven-inch kitchen knife. During his trial it was revealed that he had been watching MTV in his basement bedroom just before the killing, when a ghostly voice told him to stab his father, who was Satan. He later said that he thought he was Jesus Christ and that his real father was God. He was ultimately found not guilty by reason of insanity and has been remanded to the Northcoast Behavioral Healthcare's Northfield campus ever since.

Wellington

The home of Tim and Leslie Simonson is known throughout the community of Wellington and greater Lorain County. The majestic Italianate "painted lady" was first erected on the lot sometime between 1870 and 1871. It changed hands between several of Wellington's most prominent citizens before falling into disrepair halfway through the last century. By 1976 the Simonsons had fallen in love with the old structure, and in line with their deep commitment to preserving Wellington's past, made the decision to purchase the home and resurrect it to its former glory. Today the fully restored home stands as a source of pride for the historic community. The renovated carriage house at the rear of the property is known as the Simonson Clock Shop.

The home is said to have a bit of a haunted past—some of which has been experienced by the Simonson family. As a young boy, Tim and Leslie's son often talked of a man standing in the corner of a particular room of

Simonson House in Wellington. *From the author.*

the house. One day Tim, being something of a historian, had come across photos of some of the past residents of their historic house. While showing these images to his family, their son pointed to one of Henry O. Fifield standing on the front steps of the house and said, "That's him. That's the man in the corner."

Nearly two decades later, the boy's son, while having dinner at his grandparents' home, told them about how he sometimes sees a man standing in the corner of a room.

In addition to the family's own experiences, there have been several locals who have claimed to see a figure in the window directly above the front door of the home as they pass by. This figure is often described as a woman wearing a shroud or cloak, just standing there watching out over the street. Some observers claimed that when they tried to get a better look, the figure would dissipate into the shadows.

BIBLIOGRAPHY

Cinema Treasures. "State Theatre." http://cinematreasures.org.

The Cleveland Memory Project. "Lorain, Ohio: A Collection of Historic Snapshots of One of Cleveland's Neighbors." Cleveland State University. http://www.clevelandmemory.org.

"Dean Road Bridge." Historic Bridges. June 24, 2007. https://historicbridges.org.

Elyria Chronicle Telegram. "Flames Destroy Haunted House Near Vermilion." December 8, 1923.

Elyria Republican. "Coroner Blames Murry." August 27, 1903.

Encyclopedia of Cleveland History. "Blinky Morgan Case." Case Western Reserve University. https://case.edu.

Frary, Ihna. *Early Homes of Ohio.* Richmond, VA: Garrett and Massie, 1936.

Hilton, Don. *Murders, Mysteries and the History of Lorain County 1824–1956.* Bloomington, IN: AuthorHouse, 2018.

Jensen, Oliver. *American Heritage History of Railroads in America.* New York: Random House, 1981.

"The Joseph Swift Mansion." Ritter Public Library. https://ritterpubliclibrary.org.

The Origin of the Railroad Watch. "The Great Kipton Train Disaster." Bowers Watch and Clock Repair. http://www.bowerswatchandclockrepair.com.

Sawtell, William. *19th-Century Wellington* (blog). https://19thcenturywellington.wordpress.com.

Bibliography

Severe Weather in Ohio. "June 28, 1924: Lorain Tornado." Ohio Historical Society. http://ohsweb.ohiohistory.org.

Smith, Valerie, comp. *The History of the Lorain Lighthouse 1917–2017*. Lorain, OH: Lorain Public Library System, 2017. https://lorainlighthouse.com.

Tarrant, Rich. "Vermilion Ohio, A Good Place to Live." *Vermilion Views* (blog). http://www.vermilionohio.org.

Vayhinger, Marsha. "Noises Turn up in Ridgeville Ghost Hunt." *The Journal*. October 27, 1982.

Wellington Enterprise. "A Double Tragedy." December 10, 1890.

Willis, James A. *The Big Book of Ohio Ghost Stories*. Mechanicsburg, PA: Stockpole Books, 2013.

Woodyard, Chris. *Haunted Ohio III: Still More Ghostly Tales from the Buckeye State*. Beavercreek, OH: Kestrel Publications, 1994.

About the Author

Eric Defibaugh is a life-long resident of Lorain County and a father of three boys. An avid student of history and a passionate explorer of both natural and supernatural wonders, he has traveled extensively throughout North and Central America seeking adventure, wisdom and spiritual fulfillment. Eric is a musician, an amateur photographer and an active community volunteer. He serves his community by engaging in local politics. Together with his wife, Judy, he owns Scarlet Transportation & Adventure Tours, a tour bus company that focuses on local history and attractions in Lorain County, and all of Ohio. Growing up listening to Art Bell's *Coast to Coast* radio program, he has kept an open mind about the supernatural and has dedicated a significant amount of time to researching the stories and legends of his home state. *Haunted Lorain County* is his first book.

Visit us at
www.historypress.com